PRAISE FOR

CORPORATE *Canaries*

"If managers could read only one book, this should be it."
—Bob Bartley
Editor, Wall Street Journal
Pulitzer Prize Winner
Presidential Medal of Freedom

"What a read! I was gripped for two hours, reliving every mistake
I ever made in business."
—Jean Farinelli
Former Acting CEO, Creamer Dickson Bastford

"If managers hear these 'canary chirps,' we won't suffer any more
Enron or Tyco debacles."
—John Schaefer
*Former CEO and Staff Assistant to the President of the
United States*

"These secrets work for small business too!"
—Janet Meaker
Owner, ProMarketing Associates

"Winning takes defense and offense. Too many business books only
talk about offense. Gary Sutton solved that with these lessons."
—Craig McCaw
Pioneer to the mobile phone industry, multi-billionaire

"The trick through business ups and downs is maintaining morale and acting rationally. *Corporate Canaries* shows how."

—Martha Demski
Vice President and CFO, Vical, Retired

"I've known Gary Sutton since he was a wee PR guy chasing a hot air balloon across the country. There was nothing, other than his sense of humor and a tendency to see the world a bit more keenly than the rest of us, that suggested he would enjoy such a varied, successful career as a turnaround CEO. But we didn't know about his Grandpa Sutton and the business lessons learned in the depths of the coal mines. Grandpa Sutton would be proud of his grandson's ability to translate the 'canary' wisdoms into a successful career and share those secrets."

—John Norris
Chairman, Lennox Industries

"Riveting stories with plain talk . . . solid advice on how to strengthen your company from a guy who's been there a dozen times."

—Mary Curran
Vice President, Union Bank

"The ultimate book on business has been written and cleverly packaged. Gary Sutton is straightforward and to the point. He gives advice we can use immediately in a memorable fashion. These 'canary' lessons are seen in many companies. Gary helps us recognize and act on them, instead of relearning each time. Leave copies around your office, and see what happens."

—Giles Bateman
Cofounder, Price Club, now Costco
Former Chairman, CompUSA
(and serial survivor of multiple company crashes)

"There were moments when I forgot a 'canary,' and it cost me each time. Sutton's book gives great advice, not just on how to build business, but how to make it profitable. There's a difference. This is a critical guide."

—Bob Evans
CEO and Managing Editor, Sierra Heritage *Magazine*

"Fun reading. Management 101 yet better than an MBA. This reveals business truths. Super book."

—John Hanson
CEO, Winnebago Industries (retired)

"Simple. Insightful. Useful. Gary Sutton's *Corporate Canaries* gives entrepreneurs and managers pithy, practical, and applicable advice for avoiding catastrophes. His tactical directions bespeak the wisdom of running many startups and turnarounds."

—John Otterson
Managing Director, Silicon Valley Bank

"The 'canaries' are profound. These tales reveal everything managers must know."

—Don Drobny
Former Division President, EDS
Cofounder, Perot Systems

"Good stuff! For the ambitious, the 'Corporate Canaries' will boost careers."

—Larry Schreiber
Former Vice President, RJ Reynolds (retired)

"I love the grandpa stories and lessons. This book is splendid."

—Tom Murphy
Venture Capitalist
Former Fortune *and* Forbes *Columnist*

"These corporate canaries are treasures. What struck me is how much they apply to my business."

—Tiffany Smith
Vice President, Bernstein Investment Research &
Management

"Absolutely key to business (and life)."
—Carl Vanderwilt
Former CFO and Vice President, Federal Reserve Bank

"I've owned private businesses and run a not-for-profit. The basics in here work for both."
—Allan Shaw
Executive Director, MS Society

Corporate Canaries

*Avoid Business Disasters
with a Coal Miner's Secrets*

GARY SUTTON

NELSON BUSINESS
A Division of Thomas Nelson Publishers
Since 1798

www.thomasnelson.com

Published in Nashville, Tennessee, by Thomas Nelson, Inc.

Nelson Books titles may be purchased in bulk for educational, business, fund-raising, or sales promotional use. For information, please e-mail SpecialMarkets@ThomasNelson.com.

Library of Congress Cataloging-in-Publication Data

Sutton, Gary.
   Corporate canaries : avoid business disasters with a coal miner's secrets / Gary Sutton.
     p.   cm.
ISBN 0-7852-1299-X (hardcover)
1. Success in business.   2. Business failures—Prevention.
3. Coal mines and mining—Management—Case studies.
I. Title.

HF5386.S894   2005
657.4'03—dc22   2005021007

Printed in the United States of America
05 06 07 08 09 QKP 5 4 3 2 1

To my canary, Nancy

CONTENTS

INTRODUCTION

Ducking catastrophe is key to success.

Book after book tells how to romance customers and build a business. Speaker after speaker inspires listeners to higher performance, better service, and smarter strategies.

But none of that matters when you're bleeding.

Avoiding tragedies saves energy. When you save energy, then, and only then, boosting performance and improving service and developing effective strategies become possible.

By the way, a disaster is headed toward your company right now, only to be followed by another. That's business. That's life. *Corporate Canaries* helps you detect these threats.

Do not buy this book if you're the CEO. Anybody who's made it that far understands these tales. (We hope.) If you're a self-confident CEO, however, you might hand out copies to your team. These managers will learn more about business than you could teach by example in years. I promise you that.

In fact, this may be the first book with a guarantee.

> *This book will help managers detect a serious business problem, either in your company or in a competitor's, within a year of reading. If not, I will return your money plus a dollar.*

Just write me at the publisher, within three years of the copyright. I expect a teeny handful of letters since these five lessons have been proven again and again and again.

So just what are corporate canaries?

A century ago coal miners hung canary cages in their tunnels. The little birds went silent and dropped when poison gas seeped into the mine, before any miners were hurt, saving lives. It's the same with these corporate canaries, which tell you when a business is threatened.

Before reading *Corporate Canaries,* you might like to know where I came from.

My first CEO job was running US Press in 1980. I had no prior experience in printing. The investors suspected there was some untapped potential in their business, they hired me, and by golly, we went from $10 million in revenues to $100 million in six years. This growth was audited and reported to the Securities and Exchange Commission. More important, profits and cash flow jumped equally, averaging well above the industry. And Continental Graphics acquired us at a fancy price.

In 1987, I took over Checks To-Go, a software business. This outfit had suffered through ten straight years of losses. We turned a profit in my second month, we set industry records within a year, and the business was immediately acquired at a terrific valuation by Rocky Mountain Banknote.

Next I assumed control of Smiley Industries, an aerospace manufacturer that was choking on losses exceeding 30 percent of sales. Again, cash flow was restored in months. Publicly-traded Precision Aerotech acquired the business, at an unexpected profit for our shareholders, within two years.

From 1990 to 1995, I simultaneously worked on two separate businesses. One was Knight Protective, yet another turnaround, showing heart-stopping losses. It was laughably easy to produce a fifty-three times cash return for those shocked shareholders during my tenure as CEO. (Uh-huh, that was $53 back for every dollar of appraised value in the company.) Protection One acquired Knight in 1996.

Knight Protective recovered so easily that during this same time I cofounded another business, Teledesic. Teledesic attracted $1 billion of investment money. (Yes, that's a billion, with a *b*.) Some of these later investors were Bill Gates, AT&T, the crown prince of Saudi Arabia, Boeing, Craig McCaw, and Motorola. But I left Teledesic after five years, so I claim only a paper-thin sliver of questionable credit there. Besides, Teledesic attracted so much cash that we early dreamers got bought out in 2003 at decent markups.

After Knight Protective and Teledesic, I cofounded @Backup, a data storage company that became a darling of technology investors and corporations. I retired in 2000. @Backup was acquired in 2002 for an amount that caused me and my investors no insurmountable tax problems. At all. *Sigh.* Nobody bats a thousand.

During those CEO assignments, I also chaired Kelsey-Jenney Business College through its dramatic recovery, dabbled with Alto Waste, a garbage hauler, and extended the life of POPad International, an ill-conceived retail advertising outfit.

I usually paid myself $100,000, a pitiful salary for most CEOs. But I insisted on a chunk of each company's worthless stock. That often paid millions, so *Corporate Canaries* isn't written by another overpaid consultant who's never met a payroll or some tenured professor with untested theories.

I stayed between one and five years at each place. When each ran smooth again, I got bored. In most cases, the businesses were acquired, and I was freed to find another troubled organization.

That experience, plus Grandpa's "canary" lessons, made me something of an expert at detecting business problems.

It's my hope that the lessons in this book will help your career accelerate more smoothly than mine. My first title, you see, was editor. That meant I wrote articles for the company newspaper at Lennox. One magnificent day, I became assistant advertising manager, not quite being a real manager yet, but sneaking up on the title. And suddenly I was appointed director of marketing for commercial products, a windfall. But it meant settling in Marshalltown, Iowa. My wife and I held other hopes.

Within months, I became public relations manager for Learjet in Denver. Great job. Troubled business. Awful boss. My canary went silent. In weeks, I became the sales promotion specialist at Honeywell, a giant step backward. But with some work, I restored myself to the managerial ranks and finally became the youngest director in the entire corporation.

Later, as happens even in the best of businesses, that canary stopped chirping. Some friends and I heard the silence. We left and started a toy business. It ultimately was acquired by Fisher-Price Toys. I became their general manager on the Left Coast.

Careers rarely proceed on a straight or smooth line. The same can be said of businesses. But had I understood these corporate canaries earlier, promotions might have come quicker and my businesses done even better. This can work for you.

The following lessons help you sidestep disasters, boost morale, make more money, stress less, and put broad smiles on customers' faces.

Since retiring from my CEO positions, I've joined dozens of boards. These corporate canaries helped them avoid the everyday traps businesses stumble into.

The stories reveal common business hazards, giving five "canary" warnings, and how they destroy companies. You'll read one of Grandpa Sutton's fables at the beginning of each. His coal-mining experiences show what to watch for. You'll be surprised by the ways these stories from a century ago fit your situation now.

Notice, for example, in Chapter 4 how vacillating between open-pit and tunnel methods hurt one mining company—just as Sears vacillated seven decades later. Sears acquired Allstate Insurance and Dean Witter, setting up sales offices for Dean Witter's stockbrokers and Allstate agents in each Sears outlet.

It didn't work. Nobody wanted to buy "socks and stocks" in the same place. Putting insurance and Craftsman tools across an aisle from each other didn't enhance either.

And so, Wal-Mart emerged, undistracted by selling stocks or insurance.

In another story, Grandpa explains the problem with debt. "You can spread the beams farther apart and get the coal out faster," he says, "but the risk grows. And that's the same danger as borrowing money to grow quicker."

Enron added debt. Enron grew fast. Enron's tunnels failed.

WorldCom added debt. WorldCom grew fast. WorldCom's tunnels collapsed.

Canaries protected miners. *Corporate Canaries* protects businesses. Guaranteed.

ONE

ONE

ONE

You Can't Outgrow Losses

Eight of my cousins and I sat around Grandpa, squatting on the scrubbed and waxed linoleum. He poked at the cobs flaming in his cookstove.

"The luck was upon me," Grandpa said, "so I wrote Mother a joyful letter. I told her they gave me eleven hours of work, earning two dollar and twenty, each and every day to scramble through the tunnels, wearing packs of dynamite. Mother's landlord would read my words to her, and she'd smile at my good fortune."

Grandpa Sutton had left Ballybunion, Ireland, at age fourteen. He found work in a Harlan, Kentucky, coal mine.

Blaze McTavish owned the place. He pushed hard, never spoke gently, and didn't know how to stand still. He instructed the men to drill, blast, and shovel, drill, blast, and shovel, never detouring or studying the wall veins. McTavish believed if they dug faster and straighter, ultimately they would discover the most coal. Unlike other miners, he blasted, moving rock and soil faster, ignoring the quality of the ore.

"It's nature's game of chance, men," he explained. "She puts out thin veins of coal to fool us and hides the largest deposits elsewhere in her guts. The secret is to blast and dig far and fast so we score sooner."

They dug. They blasted. They drilled. His mine produced more rock and consumed more dynamite, drill bits, picks, rail track, and ore wagons than all others combined in Harlan County. McTavish found just enough coal to maintain the frantic digging. The workers celebrated Thanksgiving with an underground lunch and a full hour break. With twinkling eyes, Grandpa said that his turkey drumstick looked big as a shillelagh. He felt thankful, feasting seven hundred feet below the surface of his new country.

McTavish worked the miners hard but did not ignore safety. Canary cages dangled from the overhead beams every fifty paces along each tunnel. The men knew to glance at the birds as they passed. If a canary fell from its perch, they'd shout an alarm, and all would sprint to the lift, hoisting themselves up into fresh air. A tiny bird's tolerance for methane is below ours, Grandpa explained. These lifesavers signaled danger before any miners fell.

McTavish's three powder monkeys,

LISTEN FOR THE CANARY

Just like the canaries detected poison gas, our first "canary" warns when your company tries to sell its way out of losses. This is the most common cause of business failure. I'm not innocent. I urged Graphic Arts Center, our subsidiary, to boost sales. They did. Graphic Arts Center, the largest printer in the West, "blasted and dug" more printing business indiscriminately. We sold more. Losses started. My fault.

Grandpa, Liam, and Charlie, took turns loading and carrying the dynamite. Each week Grandpa worked in the shed Monday and Thursday, scrambling through the shafts Tuesday, Wednesday, Friday, and Saturday.

"So every three days, we powder monkeys rinsed our lungs with fresh air," Grandpa explained. "But the Irish Virus, that whiskey bug, infected Charlie. He'd pass out in his tent many an evening."

On the days when Charlie showed up late and hung over, Grandpa and Liam took his place, jogging to the shafts instead of walking. McTavish never noticed Charlie's absences; he just grinned at Grandpa's and Liam's pace. Charlie always snuck in by 7:00 a.m., sixty minutes late, and worked an extra hour to compensate, until 8:00 p.m.

"I be scurrying through the tunnels," Grandpa said, "and 'twas Tuesday. Me pal Liam loaded our vests." Charlie showed up on time, Grandpa explained, so the pace went steady, yet hard enough that everybody sweated through their shirts by midmorning. Grandpa stooped and lugged explosives to the second tunnel, then the first, the third, and back to the second. He repeated several cycles before lunch, each time with a few sticks of explosives, never carrying enough to collapse the whole mine, should his load accidentally blow. Each canary chirped or fluttered as he passed. Grandpa's lantern lit one wall, then the other, a stretch of ceiling, and the floor. He stooped and struggled, peering ahead.

"Probably 'twere always so," Grandpa said, "but me thick head only noticed something on that particular Tuesday." He watched McTavish himself drill the holes at the end of a tunnel during one of his deliveries. McTavish shoveled rock later the same day, after a blast, at the end of Tunnel One.

It impressed Grandpa to see an owner work alongside them, handling any job in the mine. But Grandpa also noticed several thin veins of coal lacing Tunnels One and Three. Thicker lines ringed Tunnel Two.

Liam and Grandpa discussed this finding in their boardinghouse before falling asleep. Grandpa lay under the bed, with Liam taking his turn on top of it. These coal stripes fascinated them, but they followed McTavish's instructions, ignoring the walls, drilling straight, blasting and digging, hoping to stumble across a mother lode.

Several days later, Liam, Charlie, and Grandpa talked again about how Tunnel Two showed black stripes of coal in several places. It seemed to them that these veins showed where larger deposits must exist. Some were hints, barely a finger wide. One ran from the midpoint in the south wall to the ceiling. Another circled the entire tunnel, never thickening beyond two fingers. The third stretched wider than a hand, ringing the entire tunnel. But most interesting to Grandpa, all grew bigger on the south side.

Liam reminded Grandpa that they were making so much money that they sent some home each week, and McTavish understood mining better than they. Grandpa agreed. But he kept thinking.

Grandpa got Liam and Charlie to drop an extra vest to him in the mine, placing it on the counterweight each time the cage reached bottom. This way he could deliver two loads and surface only once. Grandpa hustled. He couldn't do more in a day because delivering too fast might threaten Liam's employment and certainly Charlie's.

Blaze McTavish noticed. He wrapped a damp arm around Grandpa's shoulders after work one night, told him great things lay ahead, and invited him to dinner.

"That moment was sure to come," Grandpa said, "and with McTavish seeing my efforts, instead of me boasting, I became all the more appreciated."

They ate in the hotel dining room. Grandpa told McTavish about the coal stripes in the south wall of Tunnel Two, asking if he'd ever tried digging instead of blasting, simply following the veins. McTavish patted Grandpa's forearm, harrumphed, and complimented his productivity.

Later that night, Grandpa told Liam he had mentioned the coal stripes to McTavish.

"Mind your mouth," Liam said, "oh, please, mind your mouth. We get princely pay from McTavish. Don't be risking things."

November's temperature drop caught Charlie

by surprise. He asked Liam and Grandpa if they'd share their room, although he hadn't saved enough to pay. Liam and Grandpa felt awkward. Charlie had missed several days the previous month, forcing them to work harder to cover his absences. They turned him down, but dipped into their savings and purchased some old blankets from the hotel for Charlie's tent.

Grandpa continued double-loading dynamite, making two deliveries instead of one per surface trip. He jogged to and from the shed on top. McTavish raised him by a penny an hour. He proudly wrote his mother, reporting his pay increase, hoping again that her landlord might read his letter to her. If not, surely Father Sullivan would.

Charlie, however, missed Monday and

LISTEN FOR THE CANARY

McTavish blindly pursued the coal, just as some companies blindly pursue sales. Indiscriminately. While competitors work smarter. EDS captured billions of contracts that IBM passed by. EDS bleeds, shedding management and employees while IBM reports profits.

Tuesday, and McTavish noticed. When Charlie dragged in late Wednesday, he suggested to McTavish that they dig sideways, following the veins. McTavish fired Charlie. A James Wentworth, from London, signed on to take Charlie's place. Charlie's departure saddened Grandpa. A Brit replaced him, which agitated Grandpa.

"That wretched kingdom, fouled nest of Cromwell," Grandpa muttered, despising the British. They showed Wentworth how to pack the dynamite vest after he carried for two days. Wentworth learned where each canary cage hung and how to watch them. After several weeks, they worked comfortably as a team. Grandpa never disparaged England again.

One Sunday afternoon, Wentworth invited Grandpa and Liam to watch a steeplechase. A group of English miners from a smaller operation in Harlan County, the

> **LISTEN FOR THE CANARY**
>
> Just as Donald Trump yells "You're fired" on TV, his casinos enter bankruptcy again and again.

Bixby Mine, attended. Wentworth took care that the groups mixed carefully, betting only a penny on a horse, imbibing one half pint of ale apiece and no more, comparing mine stories.

"It would be a chore, working for Bixby," Liam said afterward.

"Aye," Wentworth replied, "there's apparently not a straight path in the place."

"But did ye notice they get more coal than we?" Grandpa asked. "And they're half our size. All digging, no blasting, just follow the veins." They fell silent.

Early Monday, Grandpa pushed the sticks into the vests while Liam and Wentworth hustled up and down the shaft. Just as Liam scrambled back to the shed, Grandpa handed him a loaded vest. Blaze McTavish scurried past, shovel over his shoulder.

"Top o' the morning, Mr. McTavish," Grandpa said. McTavish turned, waved with a smile, and marched toward the shaft.

"We've blasted all three tunnels," Grandpa added.

McTavish paused, shook a fist in the air,

and shouted: "You're the pride of that green island!"

"Might I speak with ye after hours?" Grandpa asked. Liam paled.

"Sure, laddie," McTavish replied, walking on.

"Oh, no," Liam said to Grandpa. "Let things be. We're doing just fine. Don't be turning over the cart."

Grandpa replied that he wanted to help McTavish do better. The difference, he said, would be following the veins, just like Bixby. "With our size," Grandpa said, "we could fill five trucks with black every day. No blasts, just digging."

That night, McTavish and Grandpa met at the hotel and split a pot of

LISTEN FOR THE CANARY

Had Time-Life understood this canary lesson—that you can't outgrow losses—the company never would have merged with Warner Brothers. And Time Warner wouldn't have next acquired CNN. In 2002 alone, after Time Warner merged with AOL, the shareholders lost $60 billion in stock value. Growing bigger doesn't stop losses. Digging rocks faster doesn't produce more coal.

coffee. Grandpa told McTavish what he heard from the Bixby miners. McTavish frowned, stared into his cup, and asked how many sticks were blown in his own tunnels that day. He smiled at the answer, but stopped when Grandpa suggested that their blasting might not be as productive as following the veins. McTavish left without a word.

The next morning, McTavish marched to the shed, followed by an Italian boy. He handed Grandpa a day's wages and walked him off the property. McTavish said a business could have only one leader, one policy, and one direction. As long as Blaze McTavish paid everybody's wages, he said, Blaze McTavish would command. The policies were his. Only he would set the direction.

But McTavish also handed Grandpa a letter of reference. He suggested Grandpa should do well if he'd "just learn to let the next boss be the boss."

That night Liam moaned from under the bed: "What'll ye do? What'll ye do?"

Grandpa thanked Liam for not saying, "I told you so." Grandpa mentioned that he'd saved enough to cover the next two weeks' rent. Liam said he could cover Grandpa's share for another week but had no money to spare for food.

Liam didn't sleep all night. Grandpa dozed off and on. Liam rolled out at sunrise and shuffled back to the mine. He glanced at each canary as he passed but paid no notice to the black and brown stripes on the tunnel walls. That same morning Grandpa hiked four miles to the Bixby Mine, clutching his letter of reference.

Bixby wasn't hiring.

Grandpa's landlord told him he must leave when his share of the rent went unpaid. Grandpa said he expected no more than that but pointed out where a room could be added. By attaching two exterior walls, he told the landlord, plus some shingling and a window, a sizable new room would be created. The landlord agreed, provided boards, a hammer, a pound of nails, and one crosscut saw. He paid Grandpa eight cents an hour, and Grandpa built the new unit in several weeks. It rented immediately. The landlord recovered his material cost and Grandpa's wages in three months.

"Wentworth says the Bixby Mine just hit a pocket of anthracite," Liam reported one night. "They need several miners and a carpenter."

Grandpa left before sunrise, clutching his reference letter. He waited at the gate for Bixby. This time it worked. Grandpa became Bixby's apprentice carpenter, based on the letter, his recent experience with wood, and the favorable way Bixby's English miners remembered him.

"Rather decent, for an Irish," they agreed.

Three weeks later, all McTavish workers were hoisted up early. McTavish's shoulders drooped and his voice wavered as he announced the closing of his mine. Always honorable, he managed to pay wages due, most in paper dollars and coins, but settled a few portions by giving workers the drills, buckets, and picks. His "shut your eyes, blast, and dig faster" approach had failed.

Harlan County bled. McTavish had employed many and purchased much. He simply failed to produce enough coal, despite all the blasting and digging and tons of rock moved.

It was Grandpa's turn on the bed. Grandpa could cover Liam's share of the rent for several weeks. Liam shuffled from mine to mine, getting no offers. All other mines were smaller than McTavish's and couldn't take on more than a handful of the released workers. Grandpa arranged an interview for Liam with Bixby.

Bixby didn't hire Liam.

"Liam's a nice man," Bixby explained, "and I hope you'll not begrudge me, but I can only take on the very top two or three workers. Your friend, while obviously dependable, just isn't one of the best. I am truly sorry."

"The next morning," Grandpa said, "Liam walked to Poor Fork, where he hopped a westbound boxcar on the L&N Railroad in search of brighter prospects near the American frontier. If only McTavish had realized that nobody cares how much rock you move. All that matters is the coal."

McTavish Tried to Outgrow Losses

What does the McTavish Mine failure have to do with business disasters today?

Only everything.

There are the side lessons. Grandpa hustled and worked hard. Over time, that always pays. Maybe not next week. Maybe not next year. But through any longer period, superior efforts rarely go unrewarded.

Grandpa expressed himself. That fails only with insecure management. (And you're better off learning that quickly, just as Grandpa did. He got himself fired but used his wits to come out ahead.) Liam kept quiet to avoid being fired. But because the boss wasn't listening, the business suffered, and Liam got laid off later. Agreeable but uninspired employees are expendable when times change. Times always change.

Charlie suffered soonest from his own laziness. He wasn't dependable or productive. Worse yet, Charlie tried to give advice to the boss while performing poorly, a move that usually fails and always should.

These are the obvious lessons.

A crucial fact is that more businesses go belly-up from chasing sales, instead of profits, than for any other reason. It feels good at first. Blasting all those rocks, signing all those contracts. Must be some coal in there, right? Surely those extra sales will generate big profits.

Wrong. Too often, way wrong.

You've heard the hallway talk. "If we just land this

Acme Bolt contract, imagine how much will drop to our bottom line," the VP of Sales says. The CEO's head pumps up and down, while he claps his man on the back.

Getting more sales is the *second* most important goal for any business.

The *first* goal is making sure those new sales add new profits. The VP of sales and the CEO assumed new revenues "drop to the bottom line." Sometimes they do. But new sales bring new expenses. Be sure those added costs don't make things worse.

You hear this trouble coming in other ways.

"Aggressive pricing gets us in their door," your top saleswoman announces. Funny how that rarely works. After you stoop low to get through "their" door, "they" don't let you stand up straight later. You've dropped their expectations.

Blaze McTavish assumed that frantic blasting and lots of it must inevitably lead to coal. Likewise, management assumes too often that *any* new business will boost profits.

Graphic Arts Center, a subsidiary of ours, was and still is the largest commercial printer in the West. We promoted the head of sales to CEO, and sure enough, sales and profits jumped. We applauded, and I begged for more. Sales jumped even higher, but profits vanished. It seems in stretching for those last, extra dollars, the pricing slipped, and costs jumped out of proportion to the new volume. My board urged me to take over the business and fix it. ("Urged" may be an understatement. It seemed they might "make me available to industry" if I refused.) The company recovered in two months as a shocked management group simply got smarter about the sales they accepted. Graphic Arts Center surged into record profits that same year, earning several million dollars more than ever previously recorded.

Here's what happens when a company's profits sag and management decides to cure this by adding revenue, any revenue:

1. The cost problem isn't fixed. This is all that matters, by the way.

2. To get the new business, naturally pricing is dropped or services added and terms loosened, convincing the new prospect to abandon its existing source.

3. Employees celebrate the win, and management leads them with high fives, so everybody concentrates on the new client. This ensures worse service for the existing customers. They were already suffering, by the way, as proven by the previous losses. Now those losses grow.

4. The competitor who lost this customer counter-

attacks, promising faster service than ever before, lower prices yet, and even sweeter terms.

5. Some problems surface with this new client. But since the prior vendor is already wooing back its lost account, nobody dares suggest an adjustment.

Now our company slides from inadequate profits into heart-stopping losses. Bankers and vendors notice, tightening credit. Critical supplies get short. Managers stain the armpits of their shirts before lunch. Talented employees take jobs elsewhere, perhaps with competitors, while the mediocre performers stay, glued to their chairs and glancing over their shoulders. Worrying. Not working.

But, hey, sales are up!

New business is a great thing, an important thing, and critical for success. But trying to sell your way out of profit problems only magnifies the trouble.

Fix profits first. Then add business.

Sometimes new business solves the cost problem by covering more overhead. More often new business generates unexpected expenses, making everything worse. So why doesn't everyone just reduce overhead, to make sure profits return, instead of betting on added revenues?

Well, for one thing, the folks making these decisions *are* that overhead. Many executives slip into tragedy from a desire to become bigger more than wanting to become better. That's why most acquisitions fail. That's why pursuit of new sales, ignoring margins, is a greased chute into bankruptcy.

Ironically, when management concentrates on becoming better and forgets about getting big, the company grows anyway and does so naturally. "Better," by the way, is proven by good earnings. When you have losses, your customers are telling you that you aren't so special. And going for more volume with bad margins only makes losers die faster.

That's how younger companies strangle their canaries, by grasping for sales regardless of cost.

Kelsey-Jenney Business College, when troubled, appointed me chairman. We were a private outfit, and student loans were being withdrawn by the Feds because our finances were trash, trending toward worse, thanks to the subsidized community colleges.

Community colleges began offering similar courses for a fraction of our tuition. So our government pals were undercutting us on price, using our tax dollars. They threatened to withhold Kelsey-Jenney's student loans because their community colleges took enough students away to make our financials stink. When we slipped far enough, they canceled all student loans.

But the chancellor used our asset, agility. Rather than blindly forging ahead as McTavish did, he looked for a better path and followed it. He cut the court reporting and accounting classes when "Help Wanted" ads declined for those degrees. He pushed medical technology and computer programming as demand took off for those grads. Meanwhile, the community colleges maintained their obsolete classes, so fewer of their graduates found careers that fit their studies.

Because our class cancellations matched our additions, sales went flatter than a thin crust pizza. But because we didn't dribble away energy on weak subjects, we got better at growing ones, and cash flow went from 5 percent negative to 15 percent positive in two years, getting better and better. Ninety-two percent of our students found jobs at higher pay than they had ever experienced, within six weeks of graduation.

Yippee! Our cash surplus grew. We had so much money that finally we rashly, stupidly, and ignorantly acquired another college in Los Angeles. It literally collapsed seven weeks later in the Northridge earthquake, leaving us with nothing but condemned rubble where a four-story building stood before.

I'm not suggesting earthquakes are predictable. But there was something eerie about our college's dramatic recovery, after several years of smart, hard work, then a huge leap forward in size, followed by immediate disaster. We survived, but only after several dreary years of rebuilding.

Unexpected events kill you when sales look great but profits are thin. Always expect unexpected events. These canary lessons help you and your business survive those economic dips, customer failures, and new competitors.

Older and bigger companies choose a different growth suicide. Since they've forgotten how to innovate, they acquire. Compaq buys DEC and gets bought by HP, while everybody's share of that tough market shrinks with each move. Daimler-Benz (Mercedes) acquires Chrysler, and their canaries gag.

Mercedes stood for quality. Once. Today their cars need service more often than Toyotas. I drive both. If Mercedes can't regain excellence, all their brand will mean is higher price.

AOL and Time Warner did the same thing. Not smart. And their combined value became half of what they were worth separately.

But Merrill Lynch didn't acquire anybody after Stan O'Neal took over in 2002. Merrill Lynch dropped several businesses. Smart. Revenues shrank. Profits grew. Merrill Lynch stock doubled.

Sales and size have one purpose. That one purpose is to make more profits possible. More sales can put more profits within reach, but not when a company grabs business by taking it at a loss or doing yet another ill-conceived merger. History proves most mergers lose money.

When Is Growth Dangerous?

Look at your last three years' revenues. Then check the last three years' earnings. If profit growth matches sales increases, wonderful. Toast yourself. Business is great. You're brilliant, your spouse is good-looking, and your kids are popular.

But if earnings growth is half of the sales growth, you and the business are headed for trouble. If a recession comes quickly, your company will get smarter, cut back, and squeak by. Maybe. But when that unavoidable recession comes later, all that fat will have gelled. Unnecessary expense will be enshrined in your culture. The business will perish, smudging your résumé and obliterating your stock options.

Have faith only when this problem is recognized internally, with serious plans to push profit growth over sales. Even when profits grow, if sales are increasing twice as fast, pretty soon your margins will be too thin to survive the next economic dip. Your canary's coughing.

Three decades of being CEO in six different industries left me with insufficient energy to run another business but with some unique pattern recognition. And all I can tell you upcoming managers is that economic dips may not be as frequent as the tides. But these downturns are nearly as regular as the tides.

There are other signs of overselling. Are sales commissions paid on volume or margin? Volume's bad; margin's good. Do hallway conversations discuss sales a lot and profits little? If so, that little yellow bird is wobbling on its perch and will soon be found quivering, with tiny toes pointed skyward, on its cage floor.

Recessions follow booms. Profit growth is your only protection.

What's the Cure for a Growing Company with Shrinking Profits?

At Graphic Arts Center, management saved a great business by making commissions more profit-based. The company soared to greater heights. With Kelsey-Jenney Business College, courses were dropped that were losers, and the emphasis went to the higher-margin curriculum.

When sales are growing but profits are slipping, the

cure is easy. Easy, that is, if management understands and respects the danger.

It takes 180 days to restore profits.

There are some things that you, as a manager, can and cannot do personally to solve this problem and the other problems described in the following chapters. We'll save your individual advice for the end of the book. First, let's talk about what should happen.

Get rid of commissions if they are based on sales. Replace them with commissions based on profits. Yes, there will be more debates, but you'll be arguing over a far more relevant issue. These discussions, by themselves, help refocus the business. If calculating profits is too tough, simply put higher pricing in place, and increase commissions slightly.

This cannot be an edict. Management must work with the sales force. The business needs them. Managers must go through the problem with the group, giving examples in their industry of companies that "sold their way out of business." Ask lots of questions. Spend the first month on this, letting them know that changes are coming but that the company needs their ideas.

Some wail that "customers will vanish," "we won't meet expenses," and "the bean counters have taken over." Management must listen. Sympathize without bending.

Not all the whiners will fail. Those who stay and change will become assets.

Explain that your business has two groups that create revenues: customers and parasites. Customers are those who purchase your services at a fair profit and pay on time. Parasites are those who pay late, squeeze prices, haggle over terms, and complain.

Your customers must get better service yet. Parasites must change or be exterminated.

Management should announce the new terms after the first thirty days of listening and talking. Make the deal effective in another thirty days. That'll create a small surge as your buyers and sales crew snatch orders under the old terms. Your company should also be halfway through a recruiting program to find new sales talent, equal to 20 percent of your current force. Start these fresh troops with the new pricing and commissions. At first they'll get business slowly, not knowing your markets. But they'll accelerate faster, not having any of the bad old attitudes, if you isolate them from the veterans.

It's management's job to make the change fun. Create a new contest during the first month. Give a posh weekend trip to the salesperson generating the most profit. Award several trips to those who increased their average profit the most. Have someone from accounting and operations host each member of this group. The company isn't just rewarding the stars; you're changing a culture. Recognize all in the employee newsletter, printing photos of their trips.

After two months, interview every salesperson to gauge the effects. Find the weak spots; change a price here and a minimum there, based partly on their comments and partly on financial reality. Tell all that these revisions go into effect the following month, and celebrate by announcing another contest.

Several salespeople will quit. That's excellent. The company has added enough to compensate and ended up with a more cohesive crew, losing only the giveaway artists.

Management now must keep things this way, but always with one sharp eye on the economy, so pricing is trimmed if the market demands it. Be just as ready to harvest higher margins when the economy permits that.

Voilà! Management rebuilt the company in 180 days. (Your company should simultaneously cut costs. Tips for that are in the next chapter.)

Should sales flatten while profits surge, that's just dandy. Your company is stronger. As cash builds up, management can find other paths to grow and do it smarter next time.

YOUR BUSINESS IS IN TROUBLE WHEN . . .

1. Company revenues have grown at twice the rate of net profits for three years.
2. The sales force is commissioned on volume, without regard to profit.
3. Hallway conversations are about sales, not earnings.

Your company must change the sales incentives to recapture profit growth. Add bonuses and contests to make the switch fun while challenging. Modify the system again after sixty days. Simultaneously do serious cost cutting.

TWO

TWO

Debt's a Killer

THE COBS FLICKERED in Grandpa's stove. He tossed in pine branches and laid a knotty chunk of walnut over them. Grandpa used the cheaper fuel first, we kids learned, going from cobs to soft logs, then a harder piece. He would drop a chunk of coal on top later.

He said the Bixby Mine charts looked like a plate of spaghetti, always turning, following the veins no matter where they led. While McTavish spewed out 70 percent rock and 30 percent coal, Bixby reversed that mix, producing fewer rocks and more fuel. Bixby regarded blasting as being wasteful.

Grandpa apprenticed as his carpenter. He exchanged a saw weekly for a newly sharpened tool, keeping the same hammer. Some of the shoring could be made above ground and carried down in the cage. This meant he still managed several days a week above ground, in cleaner air, feeling sunshine on his face in the summer and basking in a light haze through the rest of the year.

Bixby seemed both opportunistic and disciplined, showing Grandpa Sutton how to make money. The tunnels generated riches of coal. The miners zigged and zagged, letting the veins dictate where to dig. In so doing, the miners became experts at working corners, while the carpenters learned to shore lumber against the softer soils.

Bixby insisted that canary cages be hung every thirty paces in the mine, since they cut through a variety of strata with their winding paths.

Kentucky suffered a balmy winter in 1912. This moderate temperature stabbed Harlan County in the heart, since coal orders dropped by half. Bixby cut back to a fifty-hour week and fired a fourth of his miners. Grandpa survived the layoff, having hustled more than his coworkers. When he offered to count the picks and shovels in the tunnels each night, the company clerk, a Cherokee, accepted with enthusiasm.

Grandpa began keeping Bixby's inventory. "He who hires managers smarter than himself," Grandpa said about Bixby, "is smarter than the men he hires, if ye can puzzle through that."

Grandpa's supervisor in the mine knew how to stretch the lumber, he noted. Each new tunnel began with two feet of space between the first and second timbers. They stretched out the third timber two feet six inches. The fourth went out three feet; the fifth, three feet six inches; and so on.

"Our supervisor's thinking was that we test the earth, stretching out a wee bit each time, never knowing the limits. In this way, we watched for a section to sag, then maintained that spacing." It seemed a practical way to find a safe gap, without wasted shoring.

Until Grandpa thought it through, that was.

One Saturday evening, during the slump, Grandpa, the clerk, and Bixby tallied receipts. After they counted lumber deliveries, tool expense, salaries, coal payments, and cash, they showed a small surplus. Nobody clapped. All of them just sighed in relief. Bixby paid Grandpa, the clerk, and himself. He poured each a half jigger of whiskey.

"Mr. Bixby knew my dream was to make enough money so I could afford a family one day," Grandpa said. He hoped to raise children who might never feel poor. That lovely vision seemed far away.

"Better times shall return," Bixby said, sipping his half shot. "And you, young Sutton, have enough vinegar to reach your dreams. What do you lads see happening?" he asked.

"There's this thing we're doing," Grandpa replied, "that invites danger." He explained that the practice of stretching out the timbers, which made economic sense, could lead to trouble.

"It's smart," he said, "were the earth constant. But we toil under changing strata. The earth's pressures ahead cannot be predicted from what's behind. A dab more wood down there, spaced consistently, and the inevitable disaster might pass us by."

"Inevitable?" Bixby asked.

"We cannot push the limit forever, without

accidentally passing it one day," Grandpa replied. "Surprises come, sure as tomorrow."

Bixby nodded. They talked of the future of America and how it might catch up with the rest of the world, meaning Eur-ope in their lifetimes.

"I cut sod in the old country," Grand-pa said, "so farming might not be such a stranger to me one day."

Bixby nodded slowly.

"But I've only saved a small stake, Mr. Bixby, and I'm forever grateful for my opportunity here. You should be counting on me for several seasons."

The next week, all new timber went in at two feet six inches.

LISTEN FOR THE CANARY

That's how the second canary warning emerged. Stretching the support timbers our farther saved lumber and produced coal faster. The miner's risk is unpredictable earth. Just as borrowing helps a company grow faster, it also increases danger. The business risks are unpredictable economies and competitors. AT&T borrowed big and moved into cable TV. Now AT&T can't make money, the stock has plunged, and this weakened giant proved that borrowing cash can trash a blue chip corporation.

Grandpa's opinion mattered. He'd changed a policy, but made no fuss over it.

Early night chills yellowed the leaves that September. This change in the weather boosted their spirits. They all knew that cold weather meant people needed more fuel, adding hours of work. Grandpa cut beams, placed planks, and pushed shoring into place. The Bixby Mine corkscrewed through the Kentucky hills. The workers rejoiced at getting sixty-six hours a week again, while several new hires learned their dark trade.

Grandpa and the clerk figured out that the weight of incoming shipments revealed how many picks or shovels were inside, and they discovered some crates were short. Those shortages stopped after a few discussions with that supplier. The delivered price for anthracite jumped from $14 a ton to $20 a ton. Bixby started paying bonuses for any day over ten tons per man, and the ground vibrated from activity below. The coal dust, usually waste, was sold to farmers. They mixed it with water, creating a fuel. The mine ran one shift every Saturday.

Bixby, the clerk, and Grandpa counted the cash, bills, and inventory on Saturday nights when the mine lay quiet. On one such evening they struggled to understand why several shovels seemed unpaid for, when a muffled sound, a new noise, a kind of *whump* raised each man's head from the desktop.

They knew.

Despite never hearing that rumble before, they instantly guessed what it meant. Thankfully it was Saturday night.

" 'Twas a thunder," Grandpa said, "but from the earth instead of the sky."

All three ran to the shaft.

A black and gray cloud curled from the opening, proving what they suspected but hadn't dared to say. They stood at the mouth, listening. It lay silent.

After an hour with no more sound, Bixby and Grandpa stepped into the cage and lowered themselves. Stopping at the first two tunnels, they felt clean air and dropped to the third. Their lamps couldn't penetrate an arm's length into the murk. Both stepped from the cage, waiting until their light penetrated farther into the passage.

Walking inches at a time, pausing to listen for spilling rock, they reached the midpoint and found splintered wood under fallen stone. The lumber failed. The earth prevailed and had crushed their third tunnel.

No noises hinted at any further problems as Bixby and Grandpa slipped back into the cage and hoisted themselves up. They put one boot ahead of the other, walking to the office, slower than they had ever trod their path. The clerk reheated a pot of coffee, and they all stared out the window.

The clerk poured everybody a cup.

"What a blessing from the Lord, to collapse on a weekend," said the clerk, a loyal Methodist and a proud Cherokee.

"Protected my name," Bixby replied. "We can clear it on Monday."

"True, sir," the clerk said, "but Number Three had mostly played out."

"Right. We'll leave it be," Bixby said. He pointed at Grandpa and added, "This carpenter saw it coming, and by his suggestion, our newer tunnels are now safely braced."

"Me thoughts were but guesses, Mr. Bixby.

We'll all be thankful that hunch was proven on a Saturday night. No widows and orphans to haunt our souls," declared Grandpa.

They sipped the coffee. The clerk found a delivery receipt for the uncounted shovels. Grandpa reconciled the count against the weight of the containers delivered. Bixby paced and shook his head. Despite the cool nip in the air, sweat stained his collar. He left. The clerk and Grandpa closed the books, walked to the hotel, split a sausage, one potato, gravy, and a plate of peas, celebrating their good luck. It could have been worse. Much worse.

TWO WEEKS LATER, Grandpa had installed twenty new beams overhead, two and a half feet apart, with no variances, no matter how solid the rock appeared. Upon his last lift up that Saturday, the clerk waited for him at the top. Grandpa stepped from the cage.

"What might it be?" Grandpa asked.

"The best," the clerk replied.

"What?"

LISTEN FOR THE CANARY

In the 1980s and 1990s, two men built billion-dollar businesses. One "spaced his beams far apart," taking on massive debt. Craig McCaw dominated the fast-growing cellular phone business that way.

Paul Orfalea kept the support beams close together while expanding his Kinko's Copy Center empire, which was acquired by FedEx in 2004. Kinko's avoided borrowing excessively. Craig McCaw embraced debt.

"You're now Bixby Mine's office manager, sir," he said.

"What? Sir? I have no jacket, no collar."

"But you can count. I'm honored to work for you," the clerk said.

Bixby confirmed Grandpa's promotion with a broad smile, a few words, and a handshake. Grandpa was to watch the lumber consumed, match it against the tunnel footage, ensure enough was being placed, compare the poundage of tools against the shipping weights, and supervise the clerk's counts of picks, shovels, tubs, coal receipts, and payroll.

But first he needed to train a new carpenter. And write his mother.

Colder weather returned. For two more years, Bixby, Grandpa, and the clerk prospered, put money in their bank accounts weekly, and ate at the hotel on many a Sunday night.

Grandpa bought a house, paying cash. The clerk purchased half of his apartment building. Demand for coal stayed high, their lumber expense grew, the population of Kentucky jumped by nearly 30 percent, and no more shafts collapsed. At the end of their second year, Grandpa owned a coat, two ties, and five collars. Bixby also made him a 5 percent owner in the mine.

"The business that thrives," Grandpa said, "is the organization that peeks around the next corner."

Life grew sweet. Grandpa couldn't know it then, but as always, a new competitor would arise. Yet Bixby and Grandpa and the clerk ran a strong operation. They just might hold their own.

BIXBY SPREAD THE FIRST BEAMS TOO FAR

Companies borrowing or coal mines spacing out the beams—it's all the same.

A little debt rarely hurts a healthy business. And spacing the timbers farther apart doesn't ensure a mine collapse. But the more your company borrows and the farther apart the beams, the more certain something will crash. The only question is *when.*

A miner cannot know the pressures in the soil ahead. And the slickest managers on Wall Street, the most over-paid government economists, and the twitchiest bankers fail to forecast every recession. They celebrate good times by pretending to understand.

Bixby got lucky. His tunnel gave way late Saturday. When a recession or a nasty new competitor comes along, and they do regularly, it's not always going to be "on Saturday night." And employees will be among the victims.

Debt is your ultimate fair-weather friend. In a healthy economy, if you borrow cash to grow faster, the extra profits often cover your interest payments. But when the economy slumps, you still have to pay the interest. Then the extra revenue doesn't exist. Your cup overflows with red ink. Now the lenders control you. As they must.

Most parts of a business adjust to tough times. You order fewer supplies, saving costs. And the vendor's prices drop, reflecting the harsher economy. The company gets by. It may lay off some employees and trim benefits for others. A few employees grumble, but most are grateful for the paycheck, knowing jobs to be scarce. You restrict all travel to advance fares and use weekend layovers. Everybody drops the Marriotts and switches to Holiday Inns, renting compact cars instead of midsize. You negotiate lower long-distance rates with a new carrier.

Maybe someone even adjusts the thermostats and turns out every third light.

Ugly? Hardly. Just the kinds of adjustments that keep a business profitable through a soft year or two. It's a bit of an adventure, a reality check, getting your group back to doing some of the things you probably should have been doing all along.

But wait a minute! How do you reduce those interest payments on the loans?

Ah, there's the rub.

One way is to declare bankruptcy, wiping out shareholders. Then the successors can renegotiate the debt. Now "ugly" fits. While your vendors' pricing often drops during bad times, do the bankers become more generous?

Nope.

Lenders make money by reducing their losses. Their profit ceiling is already set by the interest rates. So when the economy gets shaky, they call in all risky loans. They chew Tums. Your banker grasps for your loose change. That's his job.

Of every cost incurred by your company, only the interest due on debt cannot be managed down. When those payments cannot be met, your company is insolvent. You may still operate, but your stock is worthless and many contracts are automatically voided. Competitors, doing their duty, will make sure the whole world hears about your difficulties.

As a youthful CEO of US Press, viewing every glass as half full, I acquired Graphic Arts Center, Franklin Press, and Rush Press, adding them to Arts & Crafts Press. We leveraged with debt. That, uh, means we didn't have the cash to pay for them. Printing happens to be a business that throws off a lot of money when managed half-decently, so we did, squeezing and redirecting each business to boost cash flows. Operating profits doubled for acquisitions in the first year, on average.

Sound great?

Not so fast.

I slipped two phrases past you, "operating profits" and "on average." Operating profits are before interest payments, among other things. Because we scrambled fast, never overpaid, and worked hard, we made those interest payments. In four years out of six, US Press showed increases in cash flow and net earnings. Twice our net earnings dropped. Our cash flow always ran positive, but surged and dipped in ways that guaranteed my pulse would never lag.

But one year, on a modest increase in sales, earnings plunged by 98 percent, barely staying positive. My salary was bigger than our profits that year, not a fact one highlights on a résumé or a subject I cared to have my board think about much. In a year of industry-wide sales declines, competitors slashing prices, and our presses sitting empty some evenings—in spite of our price cuts—all that thrill of leveraging fast growth suddenly became sickening. Worst of all, we shed several hundred employees. There was no choice. It was humiliating.

Yes, I cut my pay. That's decent symbolism but doesn't solve the problem. Don't listen for applause from the fired employees. Don't expect the board to pat your back. They want both the company and you making more money, not less.

When we rebounded, showing a terrific but bumpy five-year growth rate in profits, Wall Street came calling. Their superstar analyst asked, "How do you feel about carrying more debt than RR Donnelley? They've got thirty times your revenues."

"It's a level we're comfortable with," I replied, trying

to sound cool, with limited success. "Given our superior growth rates, we'll continue to be leveraged. Of course, that's also why we're interested in floating some stock, so we might pay down debt from time to time."

It was my first CEO job. I hadn't a clue that our borrowings topped RR Donnelley's until this woman pointed it out. Sleepless that night, I realized why, despite consistently working six long days every week and constantly outhustling competitors, our management produced terrific profits one year and plunged the next.

Debt is a long and sharp two-edged sword. Our earnings growth, averaging much better than that of the industry, was just too erratic for any stock offering, so we were acquired by Continental Graphics. This large and publicly traded printer could absorb the volatility our debt created. US Press was valued on a price paid per earnings, and our shareholders received triple Donnelley's value.

We got lucky. Our "mine collapsed on Saturday night." Life went on.

Although I understood debt from a textbook, I had never lived it, and until you've faced the near collapse of a business you care for—simply because you're overleveraged—you don't get it.

Look at other naïve companies that think debt is harmless. Pick a utility. Now that they've been deregulated, some actually managed to load up on debt so they could acquire other businesses. They expanded into stuff and overpaid. Some, like Pacific Gas and Electric, managed to go bankrupt.

A bankrupt utility, imagine that.

In spite of deregulation, they had no true competitors. An insolvent monopoly? Selling power, something people cannot do without? Broke?

Debt is one hairy monster.

AT&T proved it again. Ma Bell suffered deregulation, borrowed some money, and made acquisitions. Like any monopoly, the company thought its "management expertise" could help some of the "less sophisticated" rabble around it. Hah! Now that stock is destroyed, staying semi-aloft on nothing but memories. AT&T can't make money anymore.

Excessive borrowing is suicidal. It's like tossing a coin, double or nothing. You might even win a few flips. But that unlucky toss, reducing your business to nothing, is certain.

I was a naïve CEO at US Press. Our debt converted small gains into gigantic victories one year and turned tiny recessions into black holes the next.

Utilities and AT&T grew dumb because they were monopolies. Trained apes can make money when there's no competition for needed services. AT&T and the utilities were like the savings and loans, which tanked after their rules were loosened and the safety nets went away. They expanded their borrowings to grow the businesses and nearly all got killed. The same thing happened to European phone companies when they deregulated. British Telecom, Alcatel, Telecom Italia, Eircom (Ireland), Deutsche Telekom, and Telekom Austria became buried in debt. They borrowed big and spent dumb. They survived only because friendly governments restricted their competition. That let the phone companies gouge their customers to stay alive, covering their less-than-brilliant moves and oversized salaries.

When debt fuels your growth, your canary gasps. Soon your business will be in other hands. That little yellow bird will stop chirping and start quivering. Maybe not for several years. Maybe next month. Sooner is better, since in a few years, the delusion will have metastasized, the debt will have grown, and more tunnels will collapse upon more miners.

How Much Debt Is Too Much?

If your corporate policy is always to lease, never to buy, that's one indicator that you have too much debt. You're overleveraged. Take a look at a few leasing companies' financials. They make more money than their clients.

If your company's debt to equity is over 1:1, you have too much. You've developed a bad habit, and unless it changes, it's bye-bye birdie.

If your executive team spends more time with bankers than with customers, your canary is wheezing. Bankers loan money. That means they'll want it back, plus interest. Customers give you money to keep. So where should more time be spent? Duh. With customers. Canaries chirp when customers are visiting; they cannot be heard when lenders march through your hallways.

There are moments and situations where debt-financed growth is shrewd, under the assumption that some larger company will acquire you before the next down cycle slaughters the business. Or you want to seize a new market before others get in. This high risk takes more agility and energy than most employee groups possess. That sometimes works. But only for companies that are fleet of foot with nerves of steel.

Craig McCaw creates those kinds of companies. In 1983, he and I took a business seminar at Harvard for small company CEOs. It lasted three weeks, with sequels in 1984 and 1985.

McCaw then ran the forty-first largest cable television

company in the U.S. I was in the top one hundred printers of America. One night we prepared a case study together, dealing with a new concept called cellular phone service. Craig didn't return for the second or third year, so I forgot the slacker.

What McCaw was doing was buying the cell phone rights for every market he could. McCaw Cellular owned that business, and ten years later AT&T acquired McCaw Cellular for $14 billion. (Apparently McCaw noticed something in our case study that I overlooked.)

Ten years later, debt in another new venture kneecapped McCaw, and the poor fellow sank from a megabillionaire down to a mere multibillionaire. But McCaw is scary smart. He'll rebound, just as he has before.

Kinko was another classmate in that same group of one hundred. Named for his Afro hairdo, Paul Orfalea, aka Kinko, avoided building up debt by creating partnerships as he expanded his copy center concept, with preppy-dressed employees and well-lit, high-traffic locations. McCaw needed debt to seize a market that appeared ready to explode. He did. It worked. Kinko didn't have a totally unique concept, and a professor warned him that he was doomed since Xerox kept dropping hardware prices. Kinko stuck to his guns and also created a billion-dollar business.

Enron, WorldCom, and Tyco loaded up on debt, made it worse by hiding it, borrowed more, and died. AT&T also took on record-setting debt but kept honest books, expanded, and merely became terminally ill instead of dying.

Enron, WorldCom, Tyco, and AT&T couldn't be saved by a larger company acquiring them. Each was the largest in its field. The greater fool theory works only until the last fool becomes the owner. Then it's "game over."

For most businesses, excessive debt adds unnecessary risk. To be fair, cable news coverage and mobile phones wouldn't exist without debt. It takes gutsy pioneers to create things that the fatter, established businesses scorn. But these business pioneers take huge risks. Just like a few of our pioneers opened up the West, others absorbed arrows. For those less willing to gamble, who don't get bored with slower success, excessive debt fills their lives with anxiety. It should.

WHAT'S THE CURE FOR EXCESSIVE DEBT?

This question is a toughie. The best solution for an over-leveraged business is to sell it to a bigger business. Let the leaders of that business swallow your debt before the next recession. They can assume it and survive. You can't.

Debt is tough to fix any other way because excessive loans prove there's a culture of impatience, bravado, and addiction to risk. Nearly every solution to change runs smack-dab into those executive attitudes. But there are ways.

The first, and smartest, is to spin off a division and use the cash to pay down debt. This can be done with the current leaders, since those who are inclined toward debt are also inclined toward transactions of any kind. Their hunger for financial restructurings makes a deal like this appealing. It's what they do. Operations bore them.

Sam Walton visited two stores a day, usually alone, learning from the clerks what was selling. Bill Gates writes and tests code. Neither Wal-Mart nor Microsoft has ever incurred any meaningful debt. In a *Business Week* interview, Craig McCaw described his desire to be "the Wizard of Oz," operating from behind a curtain. Ted Turner, while a dynamic public speaker, has cowboys on his sprawling ranch who are hired to keep guests out of the areas he's roaming alone. Walton was an operator. Gates is an operator. Both avoided debt and were constantly in touch with employees and customers. McCaw and Turner are speculators, more remote from employees, leveraging everything and inventing totally new businesses.

The problem with this solution is that to pay off, it must be done during good times. That's the only moment to capture a decent price. And this executive group, feeling fat in the billfold after the sale, its history proving it needs risk, is likely to discover "a new opportunity" to plunge back into by next Thursday.

Bad times, however, make a fix possible. That's when there's no choice but to spin off something, sell it all, and take what you can get. This likely will be done by new executives, creditor-appointed. Look for recovery in the next few years, should you survive the cutbacks.

Here's how new leadership can restore the business and change the culture in two years:

1. Get all remaining management to understand that debt was the problem. Ask how many of them accurately predicted the last recession. Then show how debt risks every employee's security. Explain how it cost them their bonuses. Talk up a new program, with themes like "rock solid" and "back to basics" in the newsletter, speeches, and meetings.

2. Stop capital purchases that don't show an inarguable payback in two years. Maybe just buy nothing for a while. When a trickle of cash builds

up, negotiate faster payments on existing leases in exchange for a reduced total. Those nervous creditors should leap at this chance.

3. Keep showing employees the results on your balance sheet, and explain the effects of economic cycles on the company again. This is critical, so there's less grumbling about old desks, fewer hires, and cheaper travel. Some will not accept the tighter budgets. They'll leave. That's good. Pray that they join your competitors. Soon your company will no longer confuse spending with strength.

4. Ask managers to rank the performance of all employees. Terminate those at the bottom 20 percent. Replace only half. Establish bonuses that make it possible to earn more than before, based on profit increases and extraordinary individual accomplishments. Try awarding these bonuses monthly, getting everyone focused on immediate results. Fire supervisors who suggest rewards for average performers or balk at ranking employees.

5. Pay special bonuses for cost cuts that work, and report them in the company newsletter.

6. Edge prices up slightly.

7. Cut your vendor list by half in exchange for lower pricing.

After six months of this activity, your income statement starts to look good, and the balance sheet begins creeping, snail-like, toward respectability. Your company's finances may not be strong yet, but the culture is recovering and that matters more.

Next your company should offer a few shares of ownership to a strategic partner or critical vendor. This ought to be low key, so the prospective partners understand you're not desperate, and you can get a reasonable valuation. Make sure they're deals that will boost your margins, not just sell some stock. If this process takes another six months, that's okay because most of the emphasis should remain on the recovery, not on selling shares. As these potential investors see your numbers continuing to improve, your value only goes up.

Within a year, one of them will invest. That clears up more debt. Remember that this new shareholder must also boost your margins. That means your new partner/investor should agree to buy a volume from you at an attractive price every year as part of the deal. Or perhaps this partner is a vendor who then sells you goods at a friendlier price. Profits grow. The value of your business climbs. This also increases the value of your new partner's shares in your business, so both sides win. Your debt is down. You're back in trim.

YOUR BUSINESS IS IN TROUBLE WHEN . . .

1. Its debt to equity exceeds 1:1.
2. Equipment is always leased, never bought.
3. Executives spend more time with bankers than with customers.

The company must spin off a business. Management must stop any capital purchases that don't show clear payback within two years. Publicize the results internally and give bonuses for cost reduction ideas. Edge up pricing. Terminate the bottom 20 percent of performers, replacing only half. As results improve, sell shares to a strategic investor.

THREE

THREE

Fools Fly Blind

ALL THAT REMAINED of the cobs was a white layer of ash. The wood in Grandpa Sutton's stove glowed red, sputtering, so he shoveled a few lumps of coal on top of the flames. Grandpa paused. He pulled out his harmonica and danced a jig. We kids giggled.

Then Grandpa knelt, staring into the fire, and talked quietly about the Bixby Mine. Grandpa recalled that he, Bixby, and the clerk were stunned one morning. They stood staring over a neighboring hill.

"It was bound to happen," Bixby said. Their clerk coughed. Grandpa shook his head. They had walked this same road together every morning, not spending money for a horse or buggy yet, and always passed this slope on their way. Now the hill was fenced with workers marking the opening for a shaft.

"We've got our own good business," Grandpa replied, "and we'll tend to it." The clerk stared at the hill.

"Let's get to work," Bixby said.

"These newcomers will surely strike coal in that hill," Grandpa said, "but we'll be trucking out plenty ourselves." They hiked on and didn't glance back.

As the days passed, Bixby's miners picked, carried, shoveled, hoisted, and trucked coal at their same rate. In night conversations at the hotel, Bixby, Grandpa, and the clerk learned that the new mine owner, Malek Zrostlik, had immigrated ten years earlier. Rumors said he made a fortune on the New York docks. Zrostlik moved fast, built an office twice the size of Bixby's, and paid miners a penny more per hour.

Bixby, Grandpa, and the clerk walked the road past Zrostlik's mine daily and after a month finally met the man. Zrostlik pulled alongside the trio in his carriage and stopped. A light drizzle dampened them.

"Mr. Bixby, may I assume?" Zrostlik asked.

"And you would be Mr. Zrostlik?" Bixby replied. He introduced Grandpa and the clerk as his partners. Zrostlik jumped down, trailing cigar smoke. They all shook hands.

"There's plenty of new Kentucky home-steaders needing coal," Zrostlik said.

"Aye," Grandpa replied, "no disagreement."

"Room for us all," Bixby added. The four men discussed the out-of-state orders and the new rail lines that carried their coal west. They agreed to share a dinner soon. Zrostlik hopped back into his carriage and pulled away, spraying them with droplets of mud.

There was business for both mines, but the dinner never took place. The men met on the road several more times, always stopping to speak, courteous if not friendly. Since Zrostlik took away one or two miners from Bixby each month, a few minutes of talk always felt like plenty. Grandpa and Bixby thought Zrostlik to be a gentleman. But they couldn't ignore that his mine seemed to be growing faster than theirs while taking away labor that Bixby had trained.

In the fourth month of his operation, Zrostlik

pulled alongside the three in a new carriage with brass trim and braided leather. Zrostlik saw them and stopped.

"My fellow miners, care to ride as far as the Zrostlik hole?" he asked.

"Ah, we're flattered," Bixby said, "and a fine carriage that is. But we discuss business on these morning walks. I'll be thanking you, Mr. Zrostlik, but we'll stay afoot."

"As you wish," Zrostlik replied, pulling away. He waved from the carriage for a furlong, while the smell of his cigar hung over the road. The clerk guessed Zrostlik's new carriage cost $100. They watched as Zrostlik draped the reins over his lap, slid his left hand in an embroidered jacket pocket, and rolled his cigar with the fingers of his right.

"He's found a key to our trade," Grandpa said, "while we're none the wiser." Nobody replied. The three trudged on to their mine.

Two weeks and one day later, Bixby's and Grandpa's clerk quit, taking a position with Zrostlik. The clerk apologized. He said that with his new salary, he might be able to pay off the mortgage on his apartment building three or four years sooner. The clerk stammered that he could not afford to refuse Zrostlik's offer.

Bixby's and Grandpa's faces froze. Finally Bixby said they understood. Grandpa wished the clerk well. They gave him a bushel of apples and escorted him off their land.

It took Bixby and Grandpa several months to recover, teaching a miner who could already read and write to handle their books. The promoted man's arithmetic turned out to be nearly reliable, so with a bit of added supervision from Grandpa, no shortages or overpayments took place. They kept the coal and cash flowing. Prices were stable. Bixby and Grandpa continued to put money in their bank accounts.

Zrostlik took a half dozen more workers from Bixby and Grandpa. A few were "big shovel, no coal" malcontents. He also stole some good workers, frustrating Bixby and Grandpa, but this didn't disable them. They became skilled at training inexperienced workers, knowing they would lose a portion to Zrostlik.

On November 14, 1885, the Harlan County supervisors told Bixby that he would not get next year's contract for coal exclusively. Those orders would be evenly split between Zrostlik and Bixby. The supervisors explained that demand continued up, and Zrostlik's prices were slightly better.

"Have our deliveries ever been late?" Grandpa asked a friendly supervisor. The official admitted that Bixby's service had always been dependable, and they didn't know how Zrostlik could perform, but with the county growing so fast, splitting the business seemed politically prudent.

Bixby and Grandpa wondered if Zrostlik might be sending cigars or liquor to the supervisors but didn't know how to prove that or what the result might be if they did. They decided to simply work a little harder and try to be a little smarter and see what happened. With the county growth that year, they guessed that splitting the contract meant a 12 percent decline in sales for them, since increasing out-of-state orders replaced some of this loss.

Bixby and Grandpa put a few coins but no folding money into their bank accounts that January, February, and March. In April, when business naturally slowed, Zrostlik's carriage pulled into their yard, and their former clerk eased out. He asked them to meet that night with Zrostlik. They agreed.

"That county business is killing me," Zrostlik said over a bottle of Beaujolais. The clerk's head wobbled up and down in agreement. Zrostlik ordered filet mignon for all four, with pâté, squash purée, and wine. Bixby and Grandpa had never sampled these menu items and watched Zrostlik before eating each. They noticed their former clerk used a fork instead of a spoon and seemed comfortable handling it. The clerk also examined the wine cork. Bixby and Grandpa couldn't figure out why a cork deserved study, and the next day they couldn't remember how to pronounce the wine.

With their attitudes swinging between mistrust and opportunity, Bixby and Grandpa agreed to take over Zrostlik's business. Grandpa would run it. They would cover Zrostlik's existing debts and split any profits evenly.

Grandpa learned that Zrostlik never ordered pick handles. The clerk told him Zrostlik ordered an entire new pick each time a handle broke. Grandpa found that the drill crates were not weighed upon receipt. The clerk admitted that Zrostlik saw that practice as a waste of time. Embarrassed, the clerk said he thought he was coming to Zrostlik to learn, since the man seemed successful. But he was shocked to discover Zrostlik couldn't always pay his bills.

Together they regained control of expenses. A small windfall came when consistently short deliveries were discovered, and documented, from the shovel vendor. To keep their business, that supplier agreed to assume past shortages also had occurred. He made up the difference with overages for one year.

The Harlan County supervisors admitted deliveries from Zrostlik were tardy and agreed to a price increase, matching Bixby's. In exchange, Grandpa promised all deliveries would once again be made before sundown every day. All miners' pay was frozen, with open discussions about the reasons, while new labor would be hired at standard wages. Old miners with the higher pay could receive increases again after eighteen months, provided orders continued strong. Several left. Grandpa apologized to each, while replacing them with new hires at a penny less per hour and training them as he had done before. Even with the paltry orders of summer, it became obvious that profits should return to the Zrostlik mine that fall, so Bixby

LISTEN FOR THE CANARY

This canary lesson fits today. K-Mart couldn't give suppliers accurate sales reports by the month. Wal-Mart knows the exact daily sales of every item before midnight. Zrostlik didn't bother counting his picks or shovels and lost the mine. K-Mart went bankrupt. Wal-Mart, which didn't exist when I was a student, became the largest company in the world.

and Grandpa felt comfortable maintaining those salaries through one warm season.

Bixby doubled Grandpa's ownership. They restored half of their clerk's share after a year and would raise him again later. Zrostlik expected that his ownership should become worth something, partially recovering his investment. But he borrowed money against that expectation, maintaining his lifestyle at the hotel.

"It's less than brave and more than foolish," Grandpa said, "to drive a carriage without holding the reins." But Zrostlik ignored all business "reins" while overpaying for carriages, offices, labor, and tools.

Bixby and Grandpa had suffered a nervous year, watching this new competitor pass them by. Yet Zrostlik's progress had been a mirage. Mr. Bixby and Grandpa ran their business with sensible controls and triumphed over a flashy competitor.

"There never was a busier time under a blacker cloud," Grandpa said. During this year of stress, his mother had passed away. Father Sullivan, the same priest who had baptized Grandpa, sent him letters describing her failing health. With each message Grandpa thought about quitting and returning to his sad green island. His stomach felt full of coal, he said, worrying over business while his mother faded away.

Grandpa longed for a family, but new trouble lurked ahead.

ZROSTLIK RODE WITHOUT REINS

A century has passed since that canary lesson, and not one thing has changed. If your company has poor controls, it fails. And controls don't mean squeezing costs, just understanding them. K-Mart couldn't tell vendors how their products sold on a monthly basis with any accuracy. Wal-Mart told them precisely, daily if wanted.

Managers can control costs. Try as they might, managers cannot control revenues. Customers decide that. So manage what you can. Manage costs.

Stumbling onto a business with faulty cost controls is bliss because improvements come fast and easy. Just set up relevant yardsticks, pay attention, and act logically.

Checks To-Go produced two products. Custom forms showed a 63 percent gross margin and were tailored to fit each client. Software-compatible forms came off the shelf, with only a 38 percent gross margin.

The accounting seemed right. The general and administrative costs were allocated as a percent against each product's revenues. Proper, proper and wrong, wrong.

Listening in on customer service, we heard that

Custom Forms generated more than 90 percent of the calls. Watching order entry showed that nearly all returns and cancellations were Custom Forms. In the first week, without wasting time on decimal-point precision, we changed the overhead allocation to approximate what those costs seemed to be by product.

The company was making all its money on the Software-Compatible Forms because they suffered no returns, few cancellations, and hardly any customer service calls. Even more interesting, the "rush service" portion of that business, which comprised less than 10 percent of the orders, was generating 120 percent of the profit. Everything else was a loss.

We priced up the Custom Forms business until it went away. We converted all business to rushed orders with a modest price increase. Honest accounting showed what to do.

First profits came in that same quarter. Then came the first profitable year, followed by a year with record profits. This from a business that had run up ten years of losses, so our interest costs remained huge. Deluxe Check, a gigantic competitor, sat on a pile of cash, enjoying gains from interest, and still couldn't match our profits or growth. Best of all, there were no layoffs and only the normal cost cutting required. We even dribbled away some profits by, gulp, painting the offices.

There's power in simply understanding what generates your profits.

Sunbeam and Lucent, giant companies, both shriveled to a fraction of their previous market value. Neither used adequate controls. If they survive, it won't be pretty. Anybody who counted on Sunbeam or Lucent stock for retirement now faces an extra lifetime of work before kicking back.

Sunbeam's and Lucent's management systems left them book sales that didn't exist. So, believing their false top line, both teams let their cost lines blossom to the ultimate embarrassment of everybody. The problem with lax controls, as Sunbeam and Lucent created, is that the executives soon start worshipping their own bogus numbers.

When companies have good cost and revenue controls, trade show activity often drops, and more dollars are spent on the factory and less on office décor. You start to understand what matters. Advertising is redirected. (Yes, advertising is measurable.) More pizzas get delivered, and fewer reservations are made at restaurants with unpronounceable French names. Advance excursion fares are used at times, sometimes with Saturday night layovers. Miraculous new IT systems aren't proposed, but the existing data are put to work. Everybody earns better bonuses, the stock goes up, and customers smile again. A grateful client may even pay for lunch once in a while.

Grandpa and Bixby weighed the delivered boxes, inventoried the picks, and counted the truckloads of coal. They built in systems to ensure that costs were controlled and revenue monitored. Zrostlik didn't. Zrostlik lost.

Out of Control? Here's How You Tell

First, ask how the audit adjustments affected your revenues and earnings at year end. If revenues changed by 1 percent or earnings by 5 percent, your controls are wobbly. That yellow bird's hanging on by one, solitary wingtip feather.

If your books aren't closed within two weeks of each month end, something's wrong. If closing dates stretch out longer today from where they were a year ago, control is slipping.

If you ask three of your peers where the business makes most of its margin and you hear three different answers, the business has lost control. Everybody has to know where profits come from. Not all products, not all territories, and not all markets deserve the same amount of attention. Some are losers and need to be ignored or priced up. One thousand small decisions are made better every day when most employees understand which markets, areas, and services generate the most margin. When they have that knowledge, the company talk gets smarter:

"The delivery truck has room for only one more shipment? Send the Texas order."

"Acme's credit slipped? Sign them anyway. Our margin's big for their service."

"Our school client invited us to display at their trade show for a small fee? Forget it. They never pay on time."

Employees make superb decisions when everybody knows which products make the top dollar.

Finally, if you have no lead indicators company-wide, then you're out of control. Accounting is fine. It's necessary. But having accounting records is like standing on the stern of a boat, reporting which rocks were just missed. You've got to look ahead as well. No standard methods exist.

These indicators might be something as simple as quote activity. Daily incoming calls might predict your next month's revenue. Supplier speed and pricing tell what's happening in your world. Your customers' credit rating trends predict their future, which is your future.

If you don't have two or three forward indicators, your controls are incomplete. You're mining without canaries.

YOUR BUSINESS IS OUT OF CONTROL WHEN . . .

1. Year-end audit adjustments are more than 1 percent of revenues or 5 percent of earnings.
2. The books don't close within two weeks of the month's end.
3. When you ask employees where the company makes its best profits, nobody knows.
4. There are no lead indicators for sales.

New systems must go in. The information needs to be spread through the company, so individual decisions are made smarter.

FOUR

FOUR

Any Decision Beats No Decision

THE SHEET METAL FLUE ticked from the heat. Grandpa shook the grate. One of my younger cousins yawned while Grandpa draped a quilt over her shoulders.

"Everything changes," Grandpa said, "except the principles. Just north of Harlan County another mine had opened, a different kind of dig."

He lowered his voice while my cousin's eyes blinked, then closed.

This new mine didn't tunnel, but scraped away broad areas of dirt with a radical device, a large bucket-shaped shovel mounted on a steel arm, powered by steam. Miners envied this operation because everything happened aboveground. Some mistrusted it. The operation hired few miners, while employing many drivers, since the open pit uncovered vast sheets of coal.

"No canaries needed there," Grandpa said. "They all worked in daylight and fresh air. But Mr. Bixby and I hung canaries, of a different sort, in our brains, keeping an eye on this newfangled development."

The open pit didn't distract Grandpa or Mr. Bixby much that autumn. They concentrated on paying off the remaining debts from Zrostlik's mine. By Christmas, they owed nothing and enjoyed three months of good profits from both businesses. They expected the following year to be twice as prosperous for the combined operations. Even Zrostlik could benefit, although much of his money would go to cover the bills he ran up at the hotel.

Grandpa's share, since he now owned 10 percent of both mines, seemed certain to generate more cash than he knew what to do with, so he opened a few more bank accounts in nearby towns, spreading his risk and avoiding attention.

Their clerk paid down more of his apartment building mortgage and anticipated being debt-free in several years. This meant all the cash from rents would be his. This also assumed the coal business stayed strong. That bet seemed safe, since the local population grew slightly and the western states were booming. The clerk studied the growth rings from the hardwood trunks felled in Harlan County. They indicated that for two centuries, every warm winter had been followed by several cold years.

"But he was smart enough to know," Grandpa said, "that even this gave no guarantee. His tree ring studies provided some comfort and showed how hard a feller thinks when his future is at stake.

"Good old Zrostlik, when we showed him that weather history, just started ordering two cigars with dinner instead of one. Cuban cigars, no less." Grandpa learned that no matter how true these canary lessons are, some human behavior goes too deep to cure.

Ironically, that's why they work.

"If everybody paid heed to the canary lessons," he said, "we'd all stay strong and compete evenly. But Zrostlik, for one, just ordered better cigars. Creditors ran Zrostlik out of town."

"SOON, A NEW SITUATION confounded us," Grandpa said. He explained that a certain Sven Lindstrom III's family ran a fleet of fishing vessels, based in Stockholm. His uncle ran the business, sending Sven to America, intending to diversify into coal.

Lindstrom purchased a mine in Pennsylvania, a second in West Virginia, and began shopping around Harlan County.

The Lindstrom family also had interests in shipping freight. Their boats hauled machinery from England to America and returned full of cotton. The cotton, although baled tight, still added less weight than the machinery their ships were designed to carry. If the Lindstroms loaded coal into the bottom of the hulls, placing cotton on top, their ships could cross back to Europe with safety. They might only break even on the coal trade but gain more favorable insurance rates, making the effort worthwhile.

"We truly didn't know what to do," Grandpa said. "Lindstrom's offer to buy our mines would make Mr. Bixby, me, and our clerk rich." But they would also become employees of Lindstrom, sharing the profits for five more years as the other half of their deal.

"Just the amount paid up front was enough," Grandpa said. "But somehow those two black holes had become our lives, and we could not imagine yielding them, even if our bank accounts overflowed."

While the three agonized over Lindstrom's generous offer, they told him about the open pit to the north. All four spent the next Sunday afternoon walking its streets, listening to talk in the town restaurant and the park. They returned to Harlan County not knowing what to think about the new method, but it appeared to be going well. The clerk stayed behind, renting a room down the road from the open pit. He counted truckloads leaving and employees arriving for several days.

Lindstrom's final offer closed the deal. Bixby, Grandpa, and the clerk would receive so much cash that none would ever need to work again unless he chose to. But they could double this amount, in the following five years, by working for a split of the future profits. The Lindstrom family committed enough extra investment to expand both, probably by opening new shafts. This would keep Bixby, Grandpa, and the clerk interested, busy, and motivated. Lindstrom would spend his autumns and winters in America, traveling between his three coal investments. He would be in Sweden during springs and summers.

Lindstrom, Bixby, Grandpa, the clerk, and Zrostlik spent a slow Sunday lunch finishing the deal. Zrostlik had whispered to half of Harlan County that a sale was pending, so he was allowed to return for the negotiations without harassment from creditors. His departure might be different.

Grandpa mentioned the importance of open-pit mining and the need to consider it as a possible future move. Lindstrom chewed his upper lip. Zrostlik nudged Grandpa's shin under the table. Bixby said open-pit mining could be the future but required new capital. The clerk agreed, giving his account of the labor required and truckloads leaving. Zrostlik left the table for the bar. Lindstrom agreed that this new method deserved consideration.

Zrostlik returned and proclaimed that until more proof was seen, no changes in mining methods were necessary.

LISTEN FOR THE CANARY

When Microsoft decided online computing was real, Bill Gates refused to talk with employees for three months unless they prefaced the conversation by explaining how it related to the Internet. And he expected many conversations. That's focus. No waffling. And the company immediately shifted direction, despite being extremely profitable as it was.

Lindstrom nodded. They signed a contract that night.

Grandpa, Bixby, and the clerk had made arrangements for their banks to accept the deposits. Zrostlik's creditors seized most of his payment, but he received some cash. He bought another carriage, hired a driver, and rode out of Harlan County without announcing a destination. Some said he headed southeast. Few cared.

Lindstrom stayed that winter, traveling among Kentucky, West Virginia, and Pennsylvania. He spent a week at each investment and a week traveling between them.

On Lindstrom's return to Harlan County, Bixby, Grandpa, and the clerk met him at the hotel for dinner.

"That open-pit mine," the clerk reported, "is already twice as big as we are. Demand for coal is so strong this year that our prices should be up by $2 or $3 a ton, but they're flat because that pit produces so much."

Lindstrom nodded.

"We might be smarter to start a pit instead of that fifth shaft," Bixby stated.

"We are making money, for sure," Lindstrom said.

"But we may be looking past an opportunity," Grandpa replied.

Lindstrom agreed to consider the matter and left for West Virginia. He returned a month later.

"The open pit caught fire," Bixby reported.

"We got an extra $5 per ton," the clerk added, "the week they stopped deliveries."

Lindstrom grinned.

"But their method," Grandpa said, "makes it look like the future of mining when the land lies right."

Lindstrom's eyebrows knotted.

"I say we drill the fifth shaft now and start mining the way we know how," Bixby said.

"Shouldn't we try an open pit on that flat stretch just north of our mine?" Grandpa asked.

"That's risky," Bixby said. "We don't know how to mine that way."

"True," Grandpa replied, "but in its first season, we saw that open pit produce more coal, and cheaper, than we could ever deliver."

Lindstrom said nothing.

"What do you think, Mr. Lindstrom?" Bixby asked.

"It's your money," Grandpa added.

"Yah, a difficult question," Lindstrom said. "Surely you would grant me some time."

Lindstrom left Harlan County early that week, planning to return in one month. Bixby, Grandpa, and the clerk worked their two mines, delaying the fifth shaft or looking for open-pit sites, until Lindstrom could decide where to risk the extra money. When Lindstrom returned, they stayed late into the night at the mine office.

"Can't we try both the fifth shaft *and* the open-pit mine, spending a smaller amount on each to learn what works best?" Lindstrom asked.

"We can spend a little on the fifth shaft," the clerk said. "But it's impossible to open a pit without spending a lot. That method requires a steam shovel, so the investment is big no matter how small the effort. The open pit up north recovered from the fire and is shipping more coal every week, holding down our prices again."

"Sure, but yah, could we try an open pit with picks and shovels?" Lindstrom asked.

"Yes," Bixby replied, "but that would prove noth-ing. You only make money by scraping up truckloads from an open pit, so test-ing without the equipment would make it seem that method doesn't work. Those guys with the steam shovel keep proving it does."

LISTEN FOR THE CANARY

Compaq faced a dilemma years after inventing the first mobile PC. Within the decade, Compaq became the largest PC brand. Competition came with lower prices. Compaq didn't know what to do, did nothing, and lost the business. Years later, the company disappeared into HP. Sven Lindstrom saw competi-tion coming and risked all by doing nothing. Indecision is toxic.

"But the gamble is so, so . . ." Lindstrom said.

"Big?" Grandpa asked.

Lindstrom nodded.

"There's a larger risk," Grandpa said, "and

that be doing nothing. They're gaining on us, and we don't have either the new shaft or an open pit."

Bixby, Grandpa, and the clerk reminded Lindstrom that each risked his share of profits with him but pointed out that Lindstrom had two other coal businesses. Even in the worst case, learning how an open pit worked, bad or good, would benefit his overall understanding. Lindstrom fidgeted. He left for Stockholm without deciding, promising that upon his return next fall they would start either the fifth shaft or an open-pit mine.

Bixby retired, deciding he didn't need his share of future profits. The clerk stayed, wanting to see through the decision on open-pit mining versus traditional tunnel mining. He had already paid off his apartment building. Grandpa remained also, wanting to see if the new method would change things.

When Lindstrom returned, he told the clerk and Grandpa that the decision seemed so important to the family that they advised him to study the open-pit mine further.

"I understand," Grandpa said. "But waiting is dangerous." Grandpa resigned, taking a train to the Midwest. The clerk stayed.

In the following seasons, open-pit mines grew faster than the underground tunnels, but together both produced more and more coal. In some areas the open pits couldn't be matched, while in hill country, the shafts proved more practical. "Sven Three Sticks," as the wealthy young Swede became known, stalled the decision for two more years, finally starting another shaft and staying away from open-pit attempts. With most of his investments in rolling terrain, this decision didn't destroy his American efforts, but a downward pressure on coal pricing, caused by open-pit producers, stifled his returns. He sold the mines in Kentucky, West Virginia, and Pennsylvania at a slight loss.

The clerk made nothing extra on the sale, but with his original payment and the apartment building paid off, he had plenty. He returned in comfort to the Cherokee reservation in North Carolina, enjoying status. His tribe appreciated the clerk's skills. He encouraged and helped several members start businesses.

Grandpa, by his standards, had become wealthy.

"Business is lost by indecision," Grandpa said. "When the leader cannot describe precisely what the organization does best, the corporate canaries go silent. Every army needs a flag. The color and design of that flag don't matter. The troops just need something to march behind. And nothing destroys a business quicker than foggy direction."

Figure Out What You Do Best; Ignore All Else; Focus; Tell Everybody

Nothing's more rewarding than fixing a corporation that's confused. Giving a clear sense of direction to a troubled business unites the workers. Efficiency jumps. They start to enjoy their work, and customer satisfaction grows.

Smiley Industries made aircraft and missile parts. I assumed control after the Detroit owners couldn't stand the losses anymore.

The company simply didn't understand what it did best. Neither did I, having never been in aerospace. But the owners were losing $2 million a year on $6 million in sales, and accelerating, so they were ready for a turn-around guy like me and radical surgery.

The parts shipped by Smiley Industries ranged from $17 hinges for 747 cargo doors to $48,000 housings for MX missile guidance systems. That was a clue. It shows what happens when a small business grows, getting better and bigger in some areas, without ever dropping the lines that made it successful in the first place. When a business stretches this way, you can boost results in one of two ways:

1. Toss out the old stuff, and focus only on the new, where competition is less and the company's skills are unique, or
2. Toss out the new stuff, and go back to making money where the business did before, presuming margins remain.

With the aerospace business, we sold the contracts for all the lower-cost "blacksmith jobs" and concentrated on the high-end work, the newer technology.

The guiding statement became "Smiley Industries makes parts from exotic alloys, in non-geometric shapes that range from 18 inches to 36 inches, with accuracies of 1/10,000 of an inch."

There's a mouthful, eh?

Boring.

Cures insomnia for outsiders.

But that statement drove this business from a gasping loser to a winner in three months, without laying off employees or restructuring debt. Quote activity dropped in half, since the rep organization suddenly understood what we did best. When the reps grasped that, they got excited. No more wasted time. But instead of sending out twice as many bids and capturing only 10 percent, we competed for half as much work and won 35 percent of the bids. Volume shot up. Our canaries chirped again.

And since the company now quoted on more appropriate work, when it won a contract, it was with a smarter bid. When you're capturing only 10 percent, you're probably "winning" the ones where you made the biggest mistakes.

Xerox's troubles started about the time it decided it wasn't in the copier business and started calling itself "The Document Company." What was that? A law firm? Paper mill? From a dominant monopoly to a confused loser in two decades.

Ford announced "Quality Is Job One" and concentrated on that. Profits shot past those of General Motors.

Ford let the slogan slip away, acquiring Jaguar, Aston Martin, Land Rover, Volvo, and Mazda. And Ford's profits careened off the pavement, like an Explorer wobbling out of control on blown Firestones.

Even Home Depot, once the master of focus, stumbled once.

After the company's birth, it refused to carry pantyhose, knowing that would confuse its image. This followed a store manager's sales test, proving that $30 million of sales, with zero investment, would result if every store put in just one pantyhose kiosk, taking up less than three square feet. Home Depot, however, did nothing but sell home improvement materials and chose not to confuse the public. Home Depot's sales and profits soared.

What was Home Depot's slip?

The company moved into decor items, with the Home Depot Expo, upscale outlets with items beyond home improvement. The result? Distraction. Mild confusion. Lowe's came along, bit into Home Depot, and grew faster.

Stick to what you are. Nobody wants a Mattel pacemaker. Betty Crocker doesn't wear miniskirts. Pavarotti won't sing rap. And if they did, the public would hate it.

Is Your Organization Confused?

Here's how to tell.

Look at your mission statement, if you have one. Write one in thirty words or less if you don't. Read your employee manual. Check your ads, brochures, and Web site.

These documents should describe precisely what your company does best, as in the case of Smiley Industries. The words should be specific. "Copiers" is specific. "The Document Company" is worse than general; it says nothing. When corporate statements make egotistical claims that are broader than your sales force understands, your business is in deep trouble. Say precisely what you do best, and be proud of it.

Never say "top quality" and "lowest price" with "broadest selection." Nobody ever does all three. Few even do two. Your company should pick one and do only what sets you apart—or your canary shall cough.

If what you deliver sounds vague, you're adrift. Domino's never claimed "cheapest" or "most choices." Domino's said fast delivery. But the company said it better than that. Domino's promised "pizza in thirty minutes" to become the largest pizza-delivery company in the world. Specific goals are the best ways to attract customers and to direct employees.

Such a statement for this book might be: *"Corporate Canaries* is the first and only book showing managers how to detect potential disasters."

If you have to search for your business's statement, your company is in trouble. If your executives don't agree on this statement, along with your customers and a few trade editors, the business will not last long.

Too many businesses talk about "corporate citizenship," "meaningful employment," and "fair profits" in their messages. Hogwash. If the business is profitable, it's paying taxes. That's citizenship. Meaningful employment happens only in profitable businesses. Have you ever seen happy workers in a company that's losing money? Your statement should not be distracted by "mother, flag, or apple pie" claims.

Profits are the underlying objective of every business. Period. But to say that is to become like all other businesses, so your message must express *how* your company will get there. These words must contain a customer benefit that is specific and unique.

Your offering should be the "fastest" or the "most dependable" or the "only widget in colors" or the "widest selection" or have "limited distribution" or offer "generous financing" or have the "longest warranty." Something. Anything. Stretch for it.

"To shoot a duck," Grandpa said, "hunters aim where the bird will be next, not where it is." He meant that this direction should guide. It need not be absolutely accurate today, but it must be within reach.

"While Lindstrom was in charge," Grandpa recalled, "we waffled between tunneling and open-pit mining, losing momentum, wasting time and energy. Those who ignored open pits and just tunneled pocketed some coins. Those who ignored tunneling and dug open pits put folding money in their pockets. We dithered and hesitated and vacillated, losing out, with Lindstrom never deciding."

YOUR BUSINESS IS
IN TROUBLE WHEN . . .

1. The mission statement tries to say many things to many people.

2. Brochure and advertisement headlines don't offer specific and meaningful benefits to buyers.

3. Employees, customers, and vendors give different answers when asked what the company does best. Leadership has failed. Nondescript companies die.

FIVE

Markets Grow and Markets Die

GRANDPA DROPPED ANOTHER chunk of coal in the stove. Its door glowed a dull red. My cousins and I edged back.

He remembered stuffing his suitcase with cash, padlocking it, wrapping the suitcase in a blanket, and tying rope around the blanket.

"I rolled west on a train for St. Louis," he said, "and set out to find me a farm." Grandpa took a coach north to Iowa. He was startled by the October leaves spotting the plains in yellow, orange, and red. This ground lay flatter and the soil ran blacker and deeper, good things for the strange crops of corn and beans covering the Midwest.

Grandpa settled in Mahaska County, Iowa, staying at a boardinghouse. Once again, he split his money between four banks, each in a neighboring village. Besides the safety, each banker might then watch for opportunities that could fit Grandpa.

"My temporary board and room were in the town of Oskaloosa," Grandpa said, "but it seemed wise to hire myself out as a farmhand in the country, so I did that the first year, to learn the trade."

In the process, Grandpa discovered how little he knew of farming, particularly American crops. But more than anything, the weather startled him.

"My customary clothes froze me in January, even with two shirts under a sweater. And the summer baked the energy from me." Grandpa bought a winter coat and mittens, plus three sets of long underwear. He spent again for a straw hat in the summer.

Laboring through one season, Grandpa handled the milking, collected eggs, slopped the hogs, and tossed down hay for the cattle. Spring planting taught him about timing with the rains. Summer cultivation was a battle against weeds, chopping and pulling, walking every row, saving the soil's nutrients for the corn and beans. Fall threshing and picking paid for the year's work, as long as the grasshoppers, corn borers, blight, or hail didn't destroy the crop. If any of that pestilence struck elsewhere, prices per bushel shot up. Nature controlled this farming business, Grandpa observed, just as weather had determined coal pricing.

Vegetables would be boiled and put up in jars before snowfall. Cows or hogs would be slaughtered, salting or smoking the meat for the winter.

"I learned a lot. Mostly I saw how different American farming was from Irish sod cutting," Grandpa said.

His Oskaloosa banker mentioned that Golda Cohen, the local coal supplier, was asking around for help to manage her business. Grandpa stopped by to see Cohen, joining her the next day as an office manager.

"That was tough," Grandpa said, "choosing to risk me money on the farm dream or go back to what I knew and tuck the money away in banks. Finally it seemed like a new occupation, in a new place, piled one risk atop the other. My innards could only stand one gamble at a time."

For another year Grandpa deposited tiny amounts into each of his four banks. He felt comfortable in the coal business. Cohen praised him as a great help. Grandpa still thought farming might have a better future, and the outdoor work appealed to him. But her small mine and its shed did protect him from the winter winds and summer sun.

They had one delivery truck.

LISTEN FOR THE CANARY

Besides Kinko and McCaw, a third classmate at my seminar was Steve Sheetz. He and his brothers run a chain of convenience stores in the East. In the early 1980s, their sales were below $100 million, but they're pushing a billion today. When I talked with Steve recently, he was focused full-time on trying to figure out where the next market shift would be, what kind of business could knock them off, and he and his brothers were dedicated to creating that new business.

Grandpa joined the Grange, a farming group, and attended the evening meetings to learn what crops were paying off for his neighbors. "Just in case I could buy me a farm one day."

The following winter froze hard, but coal orders remained flat. Grandpa's boarding-house and one of the banks holding his money stopped using coal, switching to fuel oil. This new source of heat took up less space, burned cleaner, and seemed to cost about the same through a season.

"Missus Cohen, best we get into the oil business," Grandpa said. Cohen's brow furrowed. She knew some had converted to oil and none switched back. The trend seemed against coal. The high cost of new furnaces slowed down this change, which kept most people using coal until a replacement furnace was unavoidable. Iowa didn't experience much population growth. The few new homes and buildings that were constructed didn't install a coal bin and furnace. They preferred the cleanliness and space savings from oil heat.

Cohen despised oil. It seemed, well, almost immoral. She warned all who would listen that this flammable fuel might cause regrets. Some listened, some didn't, but the lack of trouble with any new installations softened her argument each season.

Grandpa offered to buy several fuel oil tanks and set up a new business with Cohen as an equal partner. Cohen just couldn't feel right about competing with her favorite fuel, coal. She graciously turned down Grandpa's offer. And Grandpa would have felt uncomfortable competing with his former boss. So after another year, Grandpa resigned and purchased a farm near Dows, due west of Mahaska County, a half day's ride by buggy.

Grandpa heard that an Ohio company, the one making most of the coal chutes, closed. It seemed no new homes or buildings were installing coal chutes, which the delivery trucks used to unload the coal into their basements.

"That 'twas a bad omen," Grandpa said.

Cohen and Grandpa stayed friends. Grandpa traveled east for Thanksgiving dinner with

Cohen each year. They kept this tradition for years. Grandpa always brought a live turkey for cleaning and baking, while Cohen covered the rest of their table.

AT AGE FORTY-TWO, GRANDPA MARRIED. "The grandest day of me life," he said.

Cohen stood as matron of honor for Grandma. Grandpa's bride had been sent from Ireland by the church, indentured for seven years to pay her passage. While crossing the Atlantic, she fell ill with consumption. Grandma started her American life in a tuberculosis sanitarium, where Grandpa delivered vegetables in winter. They married the Sunday she was released.

"Both my dreams came to be," Grandpa said. "I wish Mother could've seen the bliss. I'm thinking, somehow, she did."

Cohen thereafter came to Grandpa and Grandma's farm for Thanksgiving, only she brought the turkey while Grandma prepared the rest of their table.

Uncle Harold was born in their first year of

marriage. Uncle Eldon came next, followed by Aunt Cornelia two years later. Eugene, my father, arrived last.

Cohen remained the widowed miner. Grandpa expanded his farm to 240 acres, never taking on any debt. Cohen struggled as the use of coal declined. Grandpa said Cohen stayed sprightly because as business declined, she did more of the manual labor herself.

"Her bank account shrank, but she stood straighter and walked faster," Grandpa noticed, with as much admiration as sadness. Golda Cohen passed away two seasons after my father's birth. As trustee,

> **LISTEN FOR THE CANARY**
>
> Just like coal heat for homes died, photographic film sales are down. Kodak is terminally ill. The company's expertise has been film. Digital has eclipsed it, and Kodak doesn't have 10 percent of the expertise in electronics that the emerging competitors do in digital cameras. It recently lost money with an increase of sales. Having entered a low-margin space, they must radically change their cost structure if they expect to compete.

Grandpa traveled to Oskaloosa to settle the Cohen estate. Little was left. He sold the business, paid bills, and sent the money left over to Cohen's younger brother in Hamburg. That covered the brother's rent for two years.

"When the world changes, ye cannot fight it," Grandpa said.

COHEN'S WORLD CHANGED

Years ago, the source for music at home was a grooved, flat, black, circular thing called a record. Machines called record players put a needle in those grooves, and sounds came out.

During the "record" era, a financier called me. It seems his company owned a Valencia, California, outfit that pressed vinyl into records. Their sales were slipping because the music industry was in a slump. This business had survived the onslaught of cassette tapes, barely, and now an experimental device called a CD, short for compact disc, had emerged. The financier thought that this CD fad would pass.

I looked at the factory. I talked to some retailers and a few folks in the music industry. It became obvious that vinyl records were following closely in the tracks of the dodo bird. Dodos are long extinct, and this record factory's canaries weren't making much noise either.

Worse, there was no apparent second use for the manufacturing equipment.

But the business was still getting some sales, shrinking, and losing money, while the faithful managers clung to their hopes, unwilling to make radical change, praying that "things would get better."

"Things" never get better. Once a slide begins, it only accelerates. The best of the best turnaround managers can't fix a dying market.

A fundamental market change creates mammoth risk and some opportunity, but the probability of failure is extreme. The only hope is to bring in a dispassionate outsider. Or if you have a single leader who owns a lot of stock, there's a shot at survival. Anything less than that and management will cash their paychecks while spiraling down into that black hole, coming up first with a timid Plan B followed by stopgap Plan C followed by Plan D for Death.

Two businesses have survived fundamental changes in recent business history. They hate each other. The companies are IBM and Microsoft.

IBM recruited an outsider, Lou Gerstner, who morphed the company from a hardware business into services. It worked. Nobody on the inside possessed the dispassionate vision required for that switch. The company previously bent metal around chips, painting the cabinets blue. IBM made some of the chips; Intel and others built the rest. These boxes were called computers and ran software that outsiders often wrote. Making blue steel cabinets is not a sustainable or noticeably unique business.

Microsoft, without suffering sales dips or losses, recognized that the Internet might become real. Bill Gates transformed Microsoft from a group laughing at the Internet into true believers overnight. You know the rest.

IBM survived because the board recognized it faced a fundamental problem and hired an outsider to fix it, giving him unprecedented authority. This doesn't often happen. And IBM, unlike Microsoft, had to see sales drop and profits disappear before waking up.

Microsoft flourished because Gates recognized the threat and shifted directions forcefully, owning enough shares to care way beyond his salary.

Both companies, not coincidentally, are in high technology where change is constant. Also not coincidentally, both are marketing driven. (Nobody ever said IBM made the best computers. And Microsoft products certainly are never free of bugs.) Marketers notice first when customers start to drift away. They adjust faster.

Elsewhere we see Kodak, competing with digital photography. Digital photography has lower margins and better results than film. That board recognized the threat and recruited George Fisher from Motorola to push Kodak into the digital age. He failed. The culture was too entrenched. That was 1993. Kodak was only beginning to feel the pain. It took ten years before the company recognized that a revolution had taken place in the market.

There's *Reader's Digest,* a magazine with average subscriber age growing older by one year every year. This board brought in Tom Ryder, a brilliant publisher, who sold the office art and finally crushed its crusty ownership structure. But there's little time left for this geriatric magazine. Its death was delayed by the "You May Be a Winner" sweepstakes. Now those mailings are banned in many states.

General Motors is rebounding, but it won't last. The company is ossified. The pension benefits granted when GM was dominant guarantee higher costs forever. The company's current "success" stems more from Ford's momentary stumble than from any inspired new Chevys or Buicks.

Business schools preach that the railroads failed because they thought their mission was railroading, not transportation. That's a lofty and wrong thought. The railroads were government-granted monopolies and, therefore, unfit for any kind of halfway competitive service, like trucking or air freight.

Sears, once the supreme, unchallenged retailing powerhouse, is out-fashioned today by Nordstrom, undercut by Target, embarrassed in price comparisons with Wal-Mart or Costco, while Foot Locker, the Limited, Bed Bath and Beyond, and Midas Muffler provide better things in every niche. The nondiscount general store is no more. Sears and K-Mart planned to merge, as this was written, looking like two drowning cats clinging to each other while the whirlpool sucks them under faster.

None of these dying businesses is lucky enough to have owners or a board that recognizes how deep their problems run. Each will pluck out their canary tails one feather at a time. Attempts to fly won't be pretty.

Once I was blessed by taking over a business so traumatized that nobody believed it could survive. This situation makes change easier. Knight Protective Industries served customers in thirty-three states. This burglar alarm company had sufficient cash to meet six more payrolls, provided nothing foolish was paid for, such as rent or utilities. The products we made were overpriced and were rated as the industry's worst by AARP. Three former distributors were suing the company with great cases. But their chances of collecting a penny after a win looked slim, since we had more debts than assets. Auditors refused to certify Knight Protective as an ongoing concern. Our finance companies declined any further customers from us. Officers were stealing. I shan't risk libel by saying the board was corrupt, but I will note that one director went from our boardroom to a prison.

I did not face strong competition for this job.

Had those conditions not existed, investors wouldn't have been panicky enough for the action needed. Drastic change was required because on top of everything else, the market shifted. Average burglar alarm installations ran about $3,400 until 1990. When ADT and Brinks came out with $99 systems—and decent ones—my canary quivered.

In three months, we stopped making and installing alarms, with "an adjustment to payroll" dropping our head count from 280 to 30. We avoided the losses incurred by selling and installing and became a monitoring station only, making money but not growing.

Since we were then profitable, we started buying accounts from other dealers. Those other dealers continued to try to sell and install systems until "things got better," turning over their monitoring accounts to us for cash so they could stay alive. Then we collected the monthly fees. So we grew again.

Since we acquired their accounts at distressed prices, our number of owned accounts, generating monthly cash, skyrocketed. We guessed that the world had changed.

LISTEN FOR THE CANARY

If you're disturbed by the layoffs involved to restore this business to profitability, consider the effect on the pension fund. To keep Knight Protective going as it was, with employees doing jobs that didn't create profits, would mean that the pensioners would need to send another check for $4 million, every year, just to keep this "investment" out of bankruptcy. Ultimately that meant those ten thousand blue-collar retirees in Minneeapolis, hoping their fund would help them relax in dignity, would need to live on $400 less per year for the rest of their lives. The fired Knight Protective employees got severance and found new jobs. We helped them. The retirees got back a multiple of their $400 per year, for as long as they lived. And that pension fund was just one of thirty investments.

Our shareholders received a fifty-three times return on their investment, in cash, over a five-year period, in an industry overflowing with bankruptcies. Notice how profits drive growth, not vice versa?

That's a fifty-three times return when all investors had expected to lose everything. Unlike many outrageous claims, this one is documented since one investor, the Minneapolis Employees Retirement Fund, published its annual performance, including valuations for each investment.

It takes a toxic experience to shake a company enough so that everybody accepts radical change. Usually it's easier for an outsider to understand that the problem runs deep. Salvation requires strong leadership and crisp direction, with immediate action. Democracy dies for a while.

When you travel, notice the statues in parks. Remember the names of streets, towns, and airports. Not many are dedicated to committees. All honor determined individuals. Strong personalities change things. Committees make reports.

Is Your Market Dying?

When a market slips away, it ain't subtle. Sales shrink. No matter what you try, customers buy less. Your competitors' sales also drop. You're all losing money. When this continues for two years, it's a death spiral, not a cycle. You're toast unless you change everything. And maybe your business dies while changing anyway.

If your executives are shaking their fists at the sky, if the hallway talk is about the good old days, if your brochures show the office buildings and picture your founders and tell stories about the company history, you have joined the walking dead. Not a single customer cares about that crud.

Be careful. Some businesses combat sales drops by raising prices. So for a brief moment, revenues go up while physical volumes drop. If you work for a publication, and your revenues are growing from price increases but circulation and ad pages are slipping downward, consider a career change. Your revenues suggest growth, but the true business is shrinking.

On the other hand, if your company has oodles of cash in the bank, is cutting back sharply, and talks openly about the absolute need for total change to survive, there's a skinny hair of a tiny chance for an unlikely survival. Absent that, not a prayer.

**YOUR BUSINESS IS
IN DEEP TROUBLE WHEN . . .**

1. Sales have dropped two years in a row.
2. The competitors' sales have dropped two years in a row.
3. Nobody's making money.

SIX

SIX

The Big Lesson, Some Universal Truths, and What Managers Can and Cannot Do

CONGRATULATIONS. You've almost finished a book that doesn't offer you instant success. That, by itself, proves solid instincts reside within you, and better things lie ahead.

Most titles are hype. Walk into a bookstore. Or scan the bestseller lists. You'll see *Eat All You Want and Lose Weight,* next to *The One Minute Millionaire,* followed by *Dare to Be Great!* Those books are shelved in the nonfiction section, which is the wrong place. This book, while using my coal miner parables, gives you reality: one big lesson, some universal truths, and tips coming next on what to do when trouble approaches.

THE BIG LESSON: DEFENSE MATTERS

Nobody wins nothing with a great offense and no defense. That's brainless. In business, this means we play both defense and offense. Defense is constantly watching for the five canary threats. And by avoiding those disasters, you and your company get stronger, have the chance to play offense, and win. New opportunities come along regularly. Only the strong can grab them. Stay healthy and watch for these canaries:

1. You can't outgrow losses.
2. Debt's a killer.
3. Fools fly blind.
4. Any decision beats no decision.
5. Markets grow and markets die.

Some outfits seem to avoid all these errors. Winnebago and Websense grew fast, generating excess cash at the same time. Neither has any meaningful debt, both sit upon a quarter billion dollars, and the stock market values each at somewhat more than a billion.

Winnebago does everything it can to ensure quality, including not always leading the industry with features. The result: Winnebago leads in profits.

Websense protects Fortune 500 IT networks by filtering Web site access, catching spyware intrusions, and detecting hacking tools. Websense does this better than its competitors but isn't distracted by other business activity like them. That's why Websense leads in profits.

Both companies are in control and understand their strengths.

Seeing Universal Truths

No top managers are the same. We see this time and again. McTavish was obsessed by his belief in volume and frantic activity. He was blind to outside opinion. Strangely enough, that's the kind of personality that sometimes accomplishes great things but more often fails and is no fun to be around. Bixby was smart, listened, and built a good life. Zrostlik couldn't live within his means, so ended up without any. Lindstrom couldn't make a decision but, having inherited wealth, bumbled along. Cohen did well, yet she stayed too loyal in a dying market.

Grandpa was a visionary, but would never use such a fancy word. The most important thing he ever did was excel at his duties. That always works. Grandpa took measured risks. He decided against changing locations and careers at the same time. Grandpa stuck to what he knew when moving from Kentucky to Iowa. He switched to farming, his dream, only after getting somewhat established locally. He put his cash into several banks to avoid risk. That was smart, and all those banks failed a few years later. Grandpa had taken his cash out and owned the farm, with no debt, when the Depression struck.

Luck helps.

Grandpa spoke up to his bosses in nondisruptive and helpful ways. That usually works, but it didn't sit well with McTavish. Grandpa benefited from learning that.

Charlie also spoke up, but he was a slacker in his job. Charlie got himself fired. Management rarely listens to employees who are failing in their assigned tasks. Management shouldn't. Charlie probably died somewhere, outside, gripping a bottle. Bixby, Grandpa, and their clerk were careful with liquor. Addictions destroy more careers than incompetence.

Both the clerk and Liam were dependable employees. Liam was uninspired and the type of employee who's easily discarded when times get tough. Times get tough regularly. The clerk had a bit more ambition, made a move that looked like a promotion, but lost ground. As a proven performer, however, he rebuilt his position and ended up as a respected, comfortable tribal elder.

Grandpa and Liam covered for Charlie's morning-after tardiness. They tried but drew the line when Charlie failed to straighten himself up. That's appropriate teamwork. Support others, but expect those who stumble to get up and recover.

Widow Cohen was a good boss and partner. Her gender was irrelevant. In those earlier times, sexism faded under life's demands. My grandmother drove a tractor. To start it, she grabbed the exterior flywheel and spun it by hand.

Other prejudices were strong but faded fast. The discomfort between Irish, Scots, and English diminished with the work. The Cherokee partner was welcomed back; it took him awhile to recover financially, but recover he did. Commerce trumps bigotry.

Of these truths, the strongest is:

> *To affect any organization, the best thing any manager can do is to run his or her area well.*

When that manager performs, he or she is a candidate for more responsibility. With better results, the manager earns respect and will be heard. That's universal. When underperforming managers are listened to, the organization is sick.

Managers Can Do Something . . .

. . . For most of these situations. Not all.

First, let's figure out who you are. In school, did you raise your hand in class? When watching sports or listening to a concert, do you sometimes wish you were performing? Most important, at work have you volunteered for extra duties? Answering yes suggests that you have ambition beyond survival. So there will be things you can do when some of these situations arise.

If you couldn't say yes to any of those questions and you have no goals for work, I must preach briefly. First, recognize that all jobs are more fun and workdays whiz by faster when you're doing exceptional things. Also remember that as somebody just trying to coast, you'll inevitably be fired in the next downturn. Finding another position will be rough.

Yet everybody doesn't need to aspire to run the business and be CEO. That only leads to most employees being ultimately disappointed. But excelling, making your department proud, and becoming a candidate for other tasks to broaden your experience are better ways to get through life. This is the reality we live and work in. Effort and energy make work a joy.

Look around. Who's having fun? The energetic, pumped up, and enthusiastic? Or the unsure, negative, and halfhearted workers? You have the freedom to become either. One gets ahead. The other gets fired. It's your choice.

Let's make one distinction. Some folks take pride in running a great department and doing their job with flair. They have no ambitions beyond that. This is more than okay. It's great. These people get rewarded anyway, with promotions and changes of assignment. Even though they didn't consciously seek them.

Other employees are overtly ambitious. They want more responsibility. They don't hide it. This is okay. But there's a caution for this aggressive employee, and that's to make sure you do your own job first. And when volunteering to help with problems outside your area, do this in a nondisruptive manner. Then all's well for you and the company.

If you're content with your duties, stick to them with pride. Remember the corporate canaries. Do your tasks well. When your business faces troubles, you'll understand why and be unsurprised. And by performing, you'll prosper in the good times and survive the bad. But you may not be the manager to step in and help fix it.

If you're one of the more aggressive types, now we'll discuss how to attack each of the five problems.

1. *If sales are growing but profits are not, talk with the CEO and top sales guy about it.* Make your case for change. Be sure your own area is outperforming all others, or why should they listen? Then offer to take charge of a limited market somewhere, testing the higher margin approach. Make this an isolated market or product. Maybe it's Tennessee only or Realtors only or Minnesota only or furniture stores only. Perhaps it's galvanized buckets or casualty insurance or dental implants or Caribbean cruises or welding rods.

Just make sure it's a representative market, yet some-what isolated from the rest of your company.

Give the sales manager and president a plan for what you'll accomplish each week for the first ninety days. Then do it. Let them know. And make sure you keep your own area of duties going well or they'll pull the plug before you get a chance to show any results.

In a few months, one of two things will be true. Profits will be better for the selected market or product. In that case, you're the best one to roll out the change company-wide. The company won. You won.

Or maybe the test failed. If you were eager and gave it a good try, the company learned something. That's worth knowing, and you proved it. Slip back into your office, crank up the productivity, and there should be no harm done. Any risk worth taking can end in failure.

2. *When debt is excessive, watch and learn.* There's little you can do about this as a manager. Since debt levels reflect executive taste for risk, arguing against it puts you against their basic attitudes. Not good. Mention your concerns. Once. Then drop it.

Above all, stick with the company. Although too much debt puts a business at risk, sometimes it accelerates growth and accomplishes the unthinkable. Turner Broadcasting borrowed money and shocked the TV networks. Cellular One went into debt and proved to AT&T that there was a market for wireless. So this could be an exciting lesson if you're up for it. And a terrible loss if you quit and the business thrives.

What if it fails? Well, this happens more often than not when debt is high. But the world will understand. And the world won't blame you. If you've performed well, there's a reasonable chance the new executive team will keep you. No guarantees, but if you end up getting tossed out, you'll reconnect fast. Every competitor will be sniffing around for the best managers out of your company's failure.

3. *If controls are sloppy, it's an opportunity.* But be careful; recognize that the CEO or owner is probably

comfortable with loose operations. He or she loves driving the buggy without reins. So make the finance or accounting head your confidant, and discuss areas where profits could improve with better controls.

Better controls doesn't mean more controls. Consider eliminating some, or at least ignoring them. Develop a few forward-looking indicators besides your accounting reports. Get them all on one piece of paper in large type.

Show operations how swings in production might be smoother if everybody paid attention. Suggest to HR how fluctuations in payroll might be less volatile. Ask sales if reducing out-of-stock situations would help, and talk up how the new reports might accomplish that.

With your accounting partner, make an intelligent guess about how much profits will improve using the new controls, and get each department to buy off on this forecast.

Now sell the CEO. Offer to implement the change.

If the CEO agrees, do it, making sure your department continues to hum along nicely. Otherwise, the CEO might kill the project before it's finished, as well he should.

If the CEO disagrees, head back to your desk, and make sure your tasks are running well. If the business wobbles, dust off the plan, and pitch the CEO again next year.

4. *When direction from the top is fuzzy, it's a real opportunity for the aggressive manager.* Businesses rebound from this almost immediately. The trick is selling it internally.

If you're lucky and handle it right, the CEO will be relieved when you show him or her how to focus the business. And why. As a manager, you're in a unique position to help make this happen.

Managers can talk with customers and hear things that the leaders don't. Same for vendors. Possibly a competitor or two. Interview several trade editors to learn what's happening.

Quiz a few of your salespeople and some of the development folks. (Developers wear titles like engineers, writers, programmers, analysts, etc., whoever creates the products and services.) From those insiders and outsiders, you'll have a feel for the trends in your business, plus what your company does best and worst.

Now discuss this with accounting and operations. Accounting may spot some areas that are high margin, and operations could see areas where more focus would boost efficiencies.

From all these conversations you'll discover a few things your company is doing poorly. More importantly, a strength or a new potential will emerge. That's the company's future.

Tell your immediate superior and the CEO that you're hearing about these opportunities. Say you'd rather dig into them further before bothering them any more. Make sure they nod with approval.

Let a week or two pass, then make a presentation that builds a case for focusing your business tighter on what the company does best. Give facts. Spice it up with quotes. Suggest that while things are "okay," there's an opportunity for greater results. Gently suggest that a couple of the weaker areas may need to be dropped or sold off to capitalize on this opportunity. Keep all of this confidential, among you and your boss and the owner or CEO. It's their decision.

If they agree, you'll be part of a fundamental change. The company should do far better, and your reputation is made. There is, of course, the possibility that the move won't work. All progress involves risk. But sometimes that risk is smaller than not changing.

Should your leaders not agree, be a good sport. Impress them by doing your duties better than ever. Stuff that report in the bottom left-hand drawer of your desk, and put some tablets and paper clips on top of it. If things drift for the company the following year, or worse, resurrect the idea. If you've been productive meanwhile, maybe it'll sell this time. Since the company has languished, chances are that the new focus will bring the business back to life. The company wins. You win.

5. *If your market disappears, it's rough.* If there's one error managers make, it's leaving too quickly. Staying, when others leave, gives you some duties you might wait years to experience elsewhere. If sales drop three years in a row, that's enough experience, and you need less pain. Then go away, capitalizing on your recently broadened résumé.

For the truly courageous, there's an opportunity of never leaving until they padlock the doors. That opportunity comes from some business within the company, a service or product that by itself makes money. Take time to learn that one. Understand it. Suggest to the owners that they sell it off or set it up as a separate division, and ask to run it. Offer to take a salary cut in exchange for profit-based bonuses of some type. That's tough to refuse. And it's an opportunity you might not see in several other lifetimes.

When profits are slipping, your company shouldn't try to sell it's way out of trouble. Fix the problem first.

Adding too much debt will be toxic during the next downturn.

No business runs well without smart controls.

Decisiveness wins.
When your market changes, so must you.

Tuck this book away in your attic or the bottom drawer of your desk, pulling it out when one of these five canaries goes quiet. Read the chapter again, and you'll know what to do.

Thank You! Thank You!

Brian Hampton, editor at Nelson Books, gave superb guidance, making *Corporate Canaries* way more relevant and readable. Kyle Olund caught some embarrassing typos and clarified many phrases.

Rick Broadhead, literary agent, loved my first draft, showed it to Brian, and the result is in your hands.

Dale Steele cofounded As We Change, which went public. It was a privilege to serve on her board. Dale thought my storytelling should go into a book. She introduced me to Margret McBride, a literary agent in our village. After hearing about all the troubled businesses I've run, Margret suggested that most managers are desperate for this advice.

Ruth Mills critiqued the outline. Larry Edwards later went through the results line by line, while Rachel Laing did a final edit. Antoinette Kuritz, who runs the La Jolla Writers Conference, became enthused over *Corporate Canaries* and sent a chapter to Rick Broadhead. Antoinette also introduced me to another local, Sandra Dijkstra, who's also a renowned literary agent and encouraged the theme.

Allan Shaw, chairman of the MS Society, added critical comments. John Schaefer, a retired CEO and former assistant to the president of the United States, helped with some comments. So did Jeananne Hauswald, retired treasurer of Seagram's and a member of several public boards. Jeananne criticized the book severely, and the simplification of concepts remains not to her taste, but her comments helped. Jan Meaker, a promotional consultant and business partner, advised me on the book's markets and caught some errors early on. Phil Ensz, a top-drawer CFO, helped and nudged a few of my comments in better directions. Mark St. Clare eyeballed the financial commentary for me. My mentors, Creighton Gallaway and Tom Murphy, indirectly forged some of the underlying attitudes in the book. Financial supporters like Morgan Stanley, Quaker Oats, Allstate Ventures, Patricof & Co., American Express, DLJ, Wells Fargo, the Walton Family Trust, Goldman Sachs, the

Minneapolis Employees Retirement Fund, JP Morgan, plus a few private equity funds that prefer to remain private, provided support for my business efforts along the way, helping hatch these canaries.

Both my grandfathers deserve credit. These uneducated Irishmen struggled into respectability and helped raise me. Grandpa Sutton started even lower than portrayed in this book. He began as a ditchdigger. He ended, as written, a comfortable farmer near Iowa Falls. Mom, Dad, and I shared a duplex in Oskaloosa with a coal-mining family, providing background detail. The Grandpa in this book is a composite of those people. Some facts were bent to make the stories flow, but the truths behind each lesson remain absolute.

My wife's grandfather died before she met him, from the black lung disease, so these coal stories lurked around both sides of our family tree. Grandma Sutton lived as presented, an immigrant from Ballybunion. The converted slaver that brought her across the Atlantic was cramped, and she probably caught the consumption on board. Grandpa actually met Grandma while mopping floors in her tuberculosis sanitarium. That was his winter work when the soil froze and ditchdigging stopped.

My ancestors were rich. Not so much in money as with common sense. That's a currency that cannot be stolen, counterfeited, or deflated. I am grateful for this inheritance.

It's humbling to imagine the difficulties they overcame. Wars, diseases, famines, and the Depression devastated their world. Unlike me, they had no parental support.

Coal mining was nasty. Miners developed an independent streak that factory workers lacked since direct supervision was impossible in the tunnels where they crawled more often than walked. At first, it was the Irish against the English and Welsh; next they banded together against the incoming Italians and finally the Slavs. Ultimately a democracy of misery joined them all together, and they struck, winning slightly better wages.

Corporate Canaries comes from all that. The parables took on meaning after my decades of running businesses. Although my work covered many industries, the problems were always the same. Again and again and again. So it shall be for you and all managers.

Every business has risks. Careers face challenges. Conquer them with these corporate canaries.

—GARY SUTTON

October 2005